THE LIFE AND STRUGGLES OF AN IRISH BOY IN AMERICA

AN AUTOBIOGRAPHY

By

DAVID S. LAWLOR

CARROLL PUBLISHING COMPANY
2 Nonantum Street
NEWTON, MASSACHUSETTS

COPYRIGHT, 1936, BY MARY F. LAWLOR

PRINTED IN THE UNITED STATES OF AMERICA

Printing Statement:

Due to the very old age and scarcity of this book, many of the pages may be hard to read due to the blurring of the original text, possible missing pages, missing text and other issues beyond our control.

Because this is such an important and rare work, we believe it is best to reproduce this book regardless of its original condition.

Thank you for your understanding.

This book is dedicated to my wife, who for more than forty years has kept step with me and is still marching bravely by my side, and my four horsemen:

Sister Mary Leon of the Dominican Order
Sister Joseph Agnes of the Notre Dame Order
Sister Ephraim of the Franciscan Order
Sister Anita of St. Joseph's Order

And

to Sister Mary Paul, Franciscan, and to Sister Gertrude who for more than fifty years has worn the Franciscan livery of Our Lady.

AUTHOR'S PREFACE

"What is life, father? A struggle, my child, where the strongest lance may fail." *Longfellow.*

This is the life story of one who believes that He who gave us the birds and the bees, the flowers and the trees, meant us to be happy here.

Every incident in this book is true as far as human fallibility will permit. There is no envy, hate or bitterness.

Like most every man in the every day world seeking to make a living, I have been bruised, short changed and tricked.

But there is no desire to get even. I cannot understand how any man can ask God to forgive his trespasses when he will not forgive.

So like a good soldier, I cover my wounds and march on, leaving the exaction of penalties to God.

You will find in the story many mistakes that I have made. In every case I have followed the light that was given me. So there are no regrets. Yet only Divine wisdom knows what lay at the end of the trails not taken.

Most every man of seventy who has moved around much could tell a better story if he wished to do so, because it is life.

Newton, Mass.,
February 11, 1936.

CONTENTS

	PAGE
CHAPTER I	13

The little town of Carrick, 1865 to 1872—The Lawlors and the Carrolls—The Christian Brothers School—The Gold Sovereign—The Informer—The Berresfords—Goodbye to Tipperary—New York—Fall River—Why the house turned round and round—The cotton mills—From six in the morning until half after six at night for twenty-one cents a day—Mill life—The Granite mill fire.

CHAPTER II	35

The effort to get an education—Night school—Evening high school—I meet Mary—The gold-headed cane—The games of sixty years ago—The great Dominican—A serious view of life—I find a chum—My mother's last illness—The Sentinel asleep at his Post.

CHAPTER III	45

What the mill taught me—The Fall River Tribune—The Minister's son—Working on commission—Discharged for being too successful—The checker game—Court reporter—The curse of drunkenness—Selling advertisements for the Herald—The Globe and the big four—A piano salesman—The Catholic Advocate—Seven years on the Daily Globe.

CHAPTER IV	56

The jewelry advertisement we borrowed from the New York Journal—Pettingill and Company—What became of the twenty barrels of presents from newspaper and special agents—Munsey and the Journal—Ware of the Journal and E. A. Grozier of the Post—Moxie and Francis sarsaparilla—The whist game.

CHAPTER V	65

Shoemaker & Clark—Sage and hypnotism—A big business built on an idea and a shoe string—An offer to go to Rochester—Shoemaker and his Double Entry Bookkeeping system—A trip to Niagara, Montreal, Quebec and the Shrine of St. Anne de Beaupre—A man who kept no debit and credit account with his friends.

CONTENTS

	PAGE
CHAPTER VI	71

The five and ten king—Cherry & Webb—How a shrewd Yankee, C. T. Sherrer, built a great business from a small capital—E. S. Brown, a great merchant—A trip to New York—The Museum of Fine Arts—Men like water find a level—Great pictures and little children.

CHAPTER VII 77

Foster Stafford and his monument—The broken flywheel—The blow that broke the stone—The fabric of character—A humble curate brings a great daily newspaper to its knees—Hard times come to Fall River—Timothy Sullivan and the Stafford Mills.

CHAPTER VIII 84

Seeking advertisements in Providence for the Globe—Why Anthony Cowell, O'Gorman, the Outlet and other Providence Stores bought space in the Globe—Advertising manager of the Providence News—The advertising value of a reader to a daily—D. Russell Brown and the News—The Outlet and the Journal and Bulletin—Working under difficulties—The day of settlement.

CHAPTER IX 92

Looking for a job—C. H. Taylor and W. O. Taylor of the Boston Globe—Swift of Minneapolis—M. Lee Starke of New York—A room in Brooklyn—Light lunches—Traveling for Starke's papers—Swift reneges—Sief of the Pittsburgh Times—Business manager of the Times.

CHAPTER X 105

Why the Times did not get the advertising—Getting the facts about circulation—How the facts were used—The Post complains—How Bear found the truth—The daily campaign for advertising—I lose my job in the Times—Become advertising manager of the Ohio Baking Company—A booklet for a bakery—Gold and silver thimbles in the bread—Frank S. Baker—We write the dealers about our new loaf of bread—Gain about 700 dealers.

CHAPTER XI 119

Bread sales jump from 10,000 to 40,000 daily—The dailies give us a front page cartoon—Chicago—A similar

CONTENTS

PAGE

campaign with far different results—What the judge had to say—The president of the company lets me go—Asking a hundred men for a job—Publicity man for the Chicago Examiner—Getting automobile advertising—Paulman of the Pierce Arrow—A call to go to Boston to put on an advertising campaign for Ward-Corby Company—The president of the company and his story—The campaign—God picks a fair flower from his garden—Thompson's Spa and their rolls.

CHAPTER XII 133
Haskell and the Boston Herald—An advertising solicitor again—Making lemonade out of the lemons that are handed to you—Gale & Kent—Dismissed from the Herald—James Dayton of the Hearst papers gives me a job—Billy Freeman and the New York American—No money so we are discharged—The indignation meeting—James T. Beckwith and a trip to Boston—Capt. M. J. Deviney—Advertising manager of Fibre & Fabric—The Little Sisters of the Poor—Making a hundred dollars—Hudson and apple pie.

CHAPTER XIII 146
Sproul and I part—John H. Fahey of the Traveler and Ben Joy now of J. P. Morgan Company—Julius Mathews and his Special Agency—Work at $25.00 a week—Printers Ink, the great journal for advertisers—Mr. Gannett of Comfort—The Guardian Angel—Sibley and the Fitchburg Sentinel—Refusal of a loan of four million dollars.

CHAPTER XIV 154
James T. Beckwith gets the Herald representation—Turn down a job in New York—Work for Ben Joy—Contracts with dailies for the Mathews Service—Meet Frank Knox of the Manchester Union—Roger Sullivan and his famous 7-20-4 Cigar—William J. Pape and the Waterbury Republican—The Madonna Gonzaga—Fred Kerry of the Bacon Department Stores—Bodenwein of the New London Day—Archie McNeil and the Bridgeport Telegram—The miracle story—Robin Damon the Salem News—Moran and the Haverhill Gazette—Why men fail—James J. Storrow runs for Mayor of

Boston and I become his press agent—A chat with James M. Curley, now Governor of this state—The Boston Traveler—James C. Higgins—A part-time contract for three years with the Traveler—Alex McGregor of Houghton Dutton and Butler of the Butler Store—Mr. Winslow of the United Shoe Machinery Corp.—The Herald repudiates our contract, but settles—E. W. Preston of the Herald-Traveler.

CHAPTER XV 189
Looked over to see if I am big enough to become publisher of the Boston American—Bennett wanted me to be advertising manager of the New York Herald—My Master's House—Meet Dr. Driscoll of the Pilot and make a part-time arrangement on commission—Edward C. Donnelly and outdoor advertising—Make a part-time arrangement with Mr. Donnelly—Dr. Ellis of the Record—Eugene M. McSweeney—J. Edward Downes —A. H. Hathaway—Shuman the Clothier and S. S. Pierce—Letters in solicitation—The value of friendship —John R. Rathom of the Journal and Bulletin—Frank P. Bennett of the Cotton and Wool reporter—My Master's House brings me a trip to the far West, the Grand Canyon, Los Angeles, San Francisco, Portland, Tacoma and Seattle—Far-a-way and its owner—Keeping the faith—Vancouver, the Canadian Rockies, Minneapolis and home—My friend T. H. Cummings becomes Librarian of Cambridge—I get a raise—The doctor says take it easy—The man who did not go to church—Father George and St. Gabriel's Monastery—The Retreats—What percentage you have to get to be saved— St. Thomas and the friar—Governor Fuller and Joseph Donovan—The Canary—My Four Horsemen—The good bishop and the man who never read a book—The depression—Selling Life Insurance and Annuities for the Equitable Life—Learning a new business at sixty-six—Mary's garden—A few thoughts and a Wish.

A LETTER TO PAPE 234
MY MASTER'S HOUSE 241
THE GREATEST MOTHER IN THE WORLD. 252
THE JOURNEY OF FATHER BEPPO 268

The Life and Struggles of an Irish Boy in America

CHAPTER I

The first time my mother kissed me was in the little town of Carrick-on-Suir, County Tipperary. This is in the South of Ireland.

I assume that she kissed me because of the wonderful love that existed between us all through her life, yet I never knew her to kiss me, nor did I ever see her kiss my father, brothers or sisters, and there were nine boys and three girls. She ruled us all with love and in all the years I never heard her raise her voice.

My mother was of the princely house of the O'Carrolls of Queens County, the same house that gave to Americans the signer of the Declaration of Independence, Charles Carroll of Carrollton.

My father was also of a princely house of the same county, the O'Lawlors. My father's people I never knew, but they must have been good, because even now I can remember the prayers he taught me. He was a great worker, not only working every day but often at night and Sundays, for in a mill such as he was a directing genius of, many repairs had to be made after the ordinary day's work was done. My mother said she never heard him say that he was tired nor did I in all the years his roof sheltered me. He never had a doctor until his last illness at seventy-two, which was caused by an accident. I didn't take after my father, for I have been tired, dead tired, ten thousand times. I have stood by loom and mule, bench and lathe when I thought I would never have the strength to carry on, but He who gave life gave strength and I was able to finish the task.

My mother's people were very well to do. Her father was a gentleman farmer, owning his own acres by giving a pinch of salt or some such trifle to the landlord every year. They had occupied this farm for many generations and, as my mother said, they must have been well to do, for the six boys all wore broadcloth coats and silk hats and the six girls all had silk dresses.

The landlord came to my grandfather and told him that his second wife, a lady of the nobility of England, had found that my grandfather's farm interfered with her view of the road. He offered him a farm of equal or greater value nearby, but this was not acceptable and it led to a lawsuit, which was carried from court to court for years and was finally decided against my grandfather, but he was given damages of three or four thousand pounds.

On the day that the verdict was given in the high courts, it was in the fall of the year and the crops were all ready to harvest, a regiment of soldiers appeared, ruined the crops, burned the house and put the whole family out on the roadside.

For three days and three nights my grandfather, with a gun, waited by the roadside to kill the landlord, but my grandmother had sent three of the eldest boys with him to see that he didn't do it.

My grandfather's folks then decided to emigrate to America, but before their plans were completed there came to the town some men with posters telling of the wonderful manufacturing plant which was erected in Portlaw, County Waterford, by the Malcomson Brothers. This company manufactured cotton, linen and wool and it would be a great opportunity for people to have good positions for themselves and their children. This brought my father's and mother's families to Portlaw, and here my mother and father were married when my father was master mechanic in the mills.

When they had four children, the firm sent my father to take charge of all the machinery in the new mills at Carrick-on-Suir, some six miles from Portlaw. These mills were owned by rich Quakers and they were a law unto themselves. In case of any trouble the mill authorities were appealed to and their decision was final. If a girl felt that she was wronged by Dick or Mike or Jack, he had to marry the girl or he and all his family would be put out to starve. The married women were allowed ten days to get back to their employment after a baby came to them. If not, she and all that belonged to her would lose their places. My mother was a weaver and when her first baby was born at the end of ten days she was sent for, but she told them she would never go back and she never did. They kept the two weeks' pay that was coming to her, but they did not discharge my father because he was too valuable a man.

These Quakers were remarkable men and great manufacturers. They were known all over the world for the excellence of their product. Their own ships sailed the seas and it was the loss of these ships with their valuable cargoes that ruined them. They had to have cotton to run the mills during the Civil War and Uncle Sam's warships caught them trying to run the blockade.

Many of the old people who knew my mother very well said that she was the prettiest girl in all of Ireland. Of course, to me, she was the most beautiful girl in all the world and the only equal she could have is the girl I married and who has been my companion for more than forty years.

My earliest remembrance was the day I was to change from girls' dresses to boys' suits. I was out on the terrace watching for the tailor and I can see him now coming up the street with my clothes over his arm. Four or five of the bigger boys sitting on the wall of the terrace were talking about Adam and Eve, "If Adam and Eve had not eaten of the fruit of the forbidden tree what a wonderful time we could have had." Then one of them said, "Here comes the tailor with Davy's suit." In honor of the occasion the group took me to steal apples at Boland's farm, and all was fine until he saw us and came to chase us, two of the bigger boys taking me by the arm and dragging me along while the angry farmer was shouting, "Wait till I get ye!"

After passing five I went to the Christian Brothers' School from nine in the morning until three in the afternoon. The school seemed to me to be about 200 feet in length, divided into two sections, one for the big boys and one for the small ones. The master stood on a raised platform on one end and we were formed in circles around the room, the leading boy in one class being the teacher of the class lower down, and so followed to the primary group. The teacher surely had an eagle eye, and any scholar who wandered for a moment in thought got a blow from a belt which was thrown by the teacher who never missed his mark, and after the belt was thrown the culprit brought it back and got ten more slaps. Fine men they were, but very strict. Before school your hands were examined to see if they were clean, also your shoes to see if they were polished. If your hands were not clean you were sent out to the pump where you washed them, and when you came back they warmed them with a fine big belt. Exercises opened and closed with the Litany of the Blessed Virgin. I can remember now—"Morning Star pray for us"—and I knew that we were at the end of our work.

Now after a lapse of sixty-five years as I recite this selfsame litany, the picture of those good men comes back and I believe that many of them are saints in heaven whose special duty it is to keep a watchful eye on little boys like me.

It turned out that while these good men had pledged their lives to God, they also loved Ireland, for in the rising of '67 it was found that they were Fenians, which meant death or transportation if apprehended, so they fled, some to this country and others to France and Spain, where again they served the Master.

We paid a penny a week to go to the Christian Brothers' School. I assume that did not cover the expenses so they must have had contributions from other sources. I went to this school until I was seven; I was in the third reader when my mother told me we were going to America.

It seems that the mill in Carrick had a superintendent named Haslem and he was accused of building houses from lumber and stone owned by the company, using the company's carpenters and having the buildings put in his own name. This led to an investigation and my father being summoned as a witness said he went there as a master mechanic and not as a spy. He was ordered back to Portlaw but refused, saying he was going to America.

America the land of promise! We all looked forward to the day we were to go. It was the dream of all the young people of Ireland to go to America. Every family tried to save enough to have one son or one daughter go, knowing that this child would work and save until enough money was sent home for another to have passage money.

It was planned that my father should come first and find a home for us. I will never forget the day he left home, because mother baked a loaf of currant bread for him to take with him. She offered it to him at the station as the train was leaving and he refused to take it. I could have killed him I was so angry. Mother told me never to be angry, that it was a grievous sin, so never since that day have I lost my temper.

As we sat together, each drying the tears of the other, we never dreamed that a loaf of bread would be a great factor in my life in after years.

When my father came to this country, he landed in Boston. The first machine shop he came to he applied for work. The owner said with much heat, "No, no, there is a panic and I am letting men go instead of hiring them."

"Thank you kindly, sir," said my father, as he turned to go. The employer said, "You're from Ireland—when did you land?" "This morning, sir," answered my father.

"Whom did you work for?" was the next question.

"The Malcolmsons Brothers, sir, in Waterford and in Tipperary."

"The Malcomsons," he exclaimed, "why, they have the greatest mechanics in the world. Show me your journeymen's papers, and I will be glad to give you work."

"Here are the papers," said my father, "I was the master mechanic."

The owner grabbed him by the arm. "Hang your hat and coat right there; your pay begins from this morning." Father had a good job there, but his friends advised him to go to Fall River to work for there there would be work for the children. And the children worked in the cotton mills. All of us, seven boys and three girls, did. Two of my brothers died in infancy, so they escaped mill life.

We didn't leave until June, some two months afterward, and in that time my mother told me many of the things that happened in my childhood. It seemed I was born in a house in front of the barracks and the soldiers came over to see my father. My father was a very lovable, genial man, in whom sunlight was always shining. Everyone loved him. He had great ability and I believe was a genius in mechanics. A man who worked with him said that in his line there was no one his equal. My brother who served as a mechanical engineer said he never met a man who had the mechanical knowledge and ability my father had.

One day when my father had invented some machine the owners gave him a gold sovereign, and he showed it to all of us. It passed from hand to hand, for we never had seen gold before. I thought it was beautiful. It came back to father and he put it in his trousers' pocket and promised mother he would buy something nice for her. In the morning the gold piece was missing. It was not in his clothes, nor did a hurried search find it. All day mother looked for it and so did I and my brothers and sisters. When they came home from school we searched everywhere but there was not a trace of it. As we searched, grandmother would call from her room in her low sweet voice, "Johanna, have you found it yet?" My grandmother's boys and girls had all gone to England or America to earn a living and carry abroad the faith that St. Patrick had kindled in the hearts of their ancestors. My mother was the youngest and the favorite daughter, so my grandmother spent her last days with us. How I loved that sweet old lady! I have no memory of her being called to His Heavenly Kingdom, but she is there as sure as there are angels and saints there.

But to return to the missing sovereign. Late in the afternoon mother must have had an inspiration for she took me up in her arms and asked me if I knew where the sovereign was. I told her I did, that I had got up in the night when everybody was asleep, went into her room and took the gold piece out of father's pocket, brought it into my room and hid it under the leg of the bed.

My mother was very nice to me and she explained that taking what belonged to another was a grievous sin. She told me never to love money for money's sake for that was avarice—the most deadly of all sins. So since that time I have not coveted what did not belong to me, and I have avoided the sin of avarice. Good priests have told me since that avarice is the one sin which is the great weapon of the devil. Only a special and direct act of God can save the miser from hell.

Then she told me about the rising in '67, how a Colonel Talbot used to come to the house to see father. He went through the American war and came over to help to free Ireland. He was a Fenian and had taken the oath to the cause, but one day he betrayed the soldiers in the barracks and the men in the mills who were Fenians. Day by day there were at least half a dozen arrested and given trial, during which Colonel Talbot turned out to be a spy in the pay of the English Government. Four times the soldiers came to our house to search. My mother told me they tore the mattresses with their bayonets and broke things and made a thorough search. Every day she expected father to be arrested. Talbot had often taken me on his knee, and maybe that was the reason when all the other names were turned in my father's name was left out.

While my father was away the girl next door to us was married and of course there was a great celebration that night. Let me tell you about this—it was the aristocratic portion of the town as far as the workers were concerned. The houses were joined together. In the first house was the paymaster and the two clerks of the mills, in the second house my father and mother and children, in the third the engineer, in the fourth the boss weaver and in the fifth a minister. I do not know just where he fitted in the town; it must have been ninety-nine per cent Roman Catholic. Late in the evening when the crowd was hilarious, someone got the bright idea of disturbing the swallows who were in the eaves and they got long poles and the startled swallows made much noise as they were driven from home. The minister came out, half dressed. The boys seized him and gave him the longest and fastest run in his life.

My mother told me stories of my father in Portlaw. The famous estate of the Marquis of Beresford adjoined Portlaw and there was quite a friendship between the Marquis and my father. He was called to do many things around the estate that required mechanical knowledge. He built for the Marquis a trough and put in it a copper bowl such as we use now in our houses to keep a sufficient amount of water in the bathroom. This kept the trough just full of water for the cattle, for the copper bowl operated enough to keep it in. The people came from all around to see this wonderful trough that no matter how much the cattle drank remained full. Of course it was boxed over so that they didn't understand what it could be but a miracle.

This great estate was owned by Lady Catherine Power until Cromwell and his army conquered the people there. He gave Lady Catherine an option of marrying one of his soldiers or he would confiscate the estate. She was a very beautiful, talented woman, but she agreed to marry one of the soldiers if she could select the one. Cromwell agreed and in the morning all the soldiers were drawn up, and then Cromwell had his little joke. Lady Catherine was to select the man from his back instead of his face. She walked in review and picked the man with the finest physique and the ugliest man in the whole army. Beresford was not only ugly, but pock marked. She shrieked and fainted, and later begged to be excused from marrying such a homely man, but Cromwell was adamant, and they were married, and that was the beginning of the Beresfords. One of the Beresfords, my mother tells, filled a well on the edge of the estate where people used to come for water, and covered it with cow dung. An old woman coming with a pail dropped on her knees and prayed God to punish him. Shortly afterward he fell ill with drouth and kept asking for water, water, and my mother said that they had to run a hose to his mouth, but it was not sufficient, for he died of the drouth.

The night before we were going away the neighbors gave us a dance. Nearly the whole town was there sometime during the evening. I know I went to sleep on the settle bed while the fiddles were playing and the feet were dancing.

AN IRISH BOY IN AMERICA 23

In the morning we took the train for Cork and the young and the old were at the station to wish the Lawlors "Goodby, good luck and God bless you." The Irish cry easily, they cry for joy and for sorrow; maybe that is what keeps their hearts so soft and so warm. We were three days and three nights in Cork waiting for our ship. It rained all the time we were there, but it was a gentle rain. Every once in a while the sun would shine, and so we had a chance to see fair Cork.

The voyage lasted nine days and I had a happy and hungry time. I was always hungry, all the other boys being hungry too. I remember my mother giving her two potatoes to a couple of boys she had tucked under her wing.

We came into New York harbor one glorious morning the fourth of July, 1872. It was Sunday and they would not let us land. We could see the people going to mass so we united our prayers with theirs and thanked God for bringing us safely across the deep. This good ship on her next passage was lost at sea with all aboard. The next day we arrived at Fall River, where my father and his friends were waiting for us. My mother then had eight children, so there were ten of us, but we had a little three-room tenement in a poor apartment house near the mill. I don't know yet where she ever put us.

Two years later when I was nine, one St. Patrick's Day, my cousin's father came up to see us and he brought a jug of whiskey. Those were the days when the Irish paraded on St. Patrick's Day and everyone rushed out to see the parade, even my father and his brother-in-law. But I went to see what was in the jug, and then I remember being under the crib and the house turning around and around. My mother sat up with me for three days and three nights, fearing I would die, but I lived and from that day have had very little use for liquor. My good mother explained to me that liquor had its uses, but to beware of its abuse, always to watch it or it would destroy me, as it was another weapon the devil used to destroy souls. And she brought home to me the teachings of the Church that a drunkard could not enter the kingdom of heaven and see God. I often wonder if the men and women, young and old, who drink to excess ever stop to think that they, too, are selling their birthright—Heaven—for a mess of pottage.

We were here but a month and my father got me a job in the mule room of the granite mill at thirty-two cents a day. At that time the mill hands began work at six o'clock in the morning and worked until six-thirty at night. I helped to put bands on the new mules and then became a tuber and a doffer. After being there some three or four years instead of getting thirty-two cents a day I got twenty-one cents for doing the same job—everyone being reduced accordingly. After I had worked there ten years I got forty-eight cents a day. I could not go any further unless I became a mule spinner and that would be ten dollars and a half a week. While I was clever, being champion doffer and tuber in all the contests, the gap was too great. I would have to wait five or six years more to get the necessary strength, so my brother got me a job in the Devol mills, where I got a dollar a day making ginghams.

This business failed when I got to be a master beamer making two dollars a day, which was the greatest of all employees' jobs excepting the overseer's berth. So I went to work again at a dollar a day as apprentice to my brother, who was a master mechanic, and I served two years at the lathe, then the bench.

The superintendent ordered me discharged to cut down the expenses.

When the Devoll mills failed on the gingham they left some thirty or forty thousand dollars worth of colored warps in the chain. The reason they failed in business was that the treasurer was a friend of a Fall River doctor who thought he knew how to dye threads. All our warps had been dyed in Philadelphia, and we had gotten along famously before the local dyehouse burned the thread, and instead of one beam a day the best we could do was get off one beam a week.

A new superintendent, my cousin, came to the mill. He wanted this material used up, and of the ten beamers I was the only one who could do it. I had learned, in addition to the copper and hack system, what was known as the brush system, and the combination could work this quite successfully, so I got the job again at two dollars a day.

All day I was bending over tying threads together. I must have tied millions of knots, but at last the work was done. The superintendent gave me a place as second hand of the spool room. The pay was one dollar a day. If beaming was purgatory, this job was hell. I was to be the first in and the last out. I was to carry in my two hands about 5000 pounds of warps throughout the day, wait on spoolers, warpers and sweep up four times a day so the mill would look nice when the superintendent came through. The spool tenders, God pity them, were the hardest working girls I ever saw. Their work was always ahead of them, so feet and arms and body were going all day long. They were paid by the box, and could earn seventy cents a day. I have known in other mills where these boxes have been increased in size so as to steal ten cents from these girls. I have helped to change the gears in the slashers in other mills so that the cuts were lengthened without the weavers' knowledge and they would have to weave a cut of cloth a few yards longer for the same price. The Church teaches that there is one sin which cries to the Holy Ghost for vengeance, and that sin is to deprive the laborer of his wages. A master mechanic of thirty years' standing in the mills confirms this and said that he knew this to be true as he had done such things by orders from the officials. This is probably true of only some mills. There may have been honest mill men, probably there were, but I believe most of them were mad on the matter of production at low cost. All or nearly all the mills stole time. They were supposed to start the mill in the early years at six o'clock, later at six-thirty. They started ten minutes before the hour under the plea they had to get headway, which only took two or three minutes. They started earlier at noon. They ran until five minutes past six and so on. Always having in mind to get a little more out of the help than they were entitled to.

When I took the job of second hand I was twenty-four and weighed one hundred and seventy-five pounds. At the end of a year I weighed one hundred and thirty-three, but I had a good boss. He had the reputation of getting the greatest production of any man in his line—that is in the warping, slashing, spooling and drawing-in. I asked him why—what was the reason for his success, why the help were attracted to him, because the best help came from miles around to work for him while the other overseers had to take what they could get. He explained that a man who went looking for trouble always found it, nagged his help, his help hated him, while those who worked for my boss loved him. He said the secret was not to see too damn much and to only see the essentials. It is forty-five years since I left the mill and I have worked for many men in many institutions. My business as an advertising man has carried me into thousands of places, and I see that Tom O'Connell was right. The man who saw only the essential things was a success and the man who saw too much was a failure.

At the end of the year in the spool room Tom O'Connell said to the superintendent, "Tim, for the love of God, why don't you do something for Dave? Here's a young fellow straight, honest, square as they make 'em, a wonderful worker and a young man of brilliant mind, and you have kept him here for a dollar a day. Shame on you!"

The next day I was appointed second hand, that is assistant to the overseer in the weave room, at eight dollars per week, but my health was gone—I was on the verge of nervous prostration. The sudden change from the quiet of the spool room to the thousand looms striking two hundred and forty times a minute was too much for me. All night long the looms all assembled under my pillow and through the night they banged, banged, banged. I didn't get a wink of sleep. Then I resolved to quit the mill forever. I went to Central Falls to see my brother and he and his good wife kept me until I regained my health.

The ordinary mill of a thousand looms, such as the Granite Mill, is about four hundred feet long and the width of a pair of mules with an alley on each side, so I would say about one hundred and twenty-five feet wide. These mills were six stories high, each story being about fifteen feet, and in the early days had a peaked roof.

There are about one hundred and five cotton mills in Fall River. All the mills look much alike. Most of them are built of granite quarried out of the bosom of the city. Some of the older mills are of brick. In the center of many of the wills is a tower enclosing the stairways to the various rooms. Some of the later erected mills left out the towers and put the stairways at the end of the mills, thus economizing space. Every mill has a three-story ell in which is the engine room with its great wheel. This carries the main belt which conveys power to the entire mill.

The two lower floors are the weave rooms containing about five hundred looms each. The third floor has the card room, the fourth and fifth the mule rooms, and the sixth the spooling, warping and slashing. This was the arrangement when I was a boy and it is much the same today, except that the mules have been replaced by the spinning frames. In the ordinary sized mill there were employed five hundred men, women and children. The average pay in my time was six dollars and sixty cents a week. We were paid monthly, that is, every four weeks, except four times a year we would get paid after five weeks. Nearly everyone was always short of money. All the grocery stores gave credit. We had a pass book like everyone else. When a purchase was made it was entered in the book. When pay day came there was a settlement or a near settlement and everyone was broke again. Then a strike or a lockout would come on and nobody would pay the grocer and he would go broke. Every pay day mother would give me ten cents from my envelope for spending money and that had to last until next pay day.

In my seventeen years in the mills I worked in every department of the mill except the card room, but my work in the machine shop made me familiar with every piece of machinery in that room and the work done by the men and women operators.

From the time I was seven till I was seventeen I spent in the mule room except three periods of three months each when I went to school. A mule spinner looked after two mules. Each mule controlled about one thousand spindles. The mule would travel out on steel tracks, which resembled in a small way railroad tracks, a distance of about five feet. The spindles turning about ten thousand times a minute. Thus the thread was made from the drawing of the rolls and the twisting of the spindles. At the end of the run the mule would reverse and wind the thread on the cop. The spinner's work was to piece the broken threads. This kept him on the jump all day when the cotton was good, but when the mill treasurer bought inferior cotton the work was very hard. I remember one spinner calling to another, "Hey, Jack, a nigger's pair of boots just came through; I expect very soon the nigger himself will come along."

We boys were assistants to the spinners; we kept the ropen in back of the mule. It was from this the thread was spun. We took off the full cops and put on the tubes for another beginning. We took away the full boxes of yarn and weighed them, for each man was paid by piece work. Those men were always kind to me. I was always nice to them and as helpful as could be. Many another boy got a blow of the fist or a kick that would make him reel were he negligent in his duties or uncivil in his remarks.

In the mill we wore, the boys and men, a pair of overalls and a calico shirt. The overalls were always rolled to the knee and the sleeves in the calico shirt were rolled as far as they could go. The shirt opened at the neck and that was what we wore summer and winter in the mill and summers outside as well as inside.

The women operatives on the street all had shawls

over their heads. A skirt, waist and shoes and she was equipped to do her work. Few of the men had overcoats or underwear. I think I was seventeen before I got an overcoat. In winter I was never warm except in the mill or in front of the kitchen fire.

The employees were all English and Irish, and these English and Irish got along just as though they were born neighbors, and in all the years in the mill I never heard a word or a fight between them. They were fine, decent, honest men. Their conversation was as a rule pure; seldom you heard an immodest story. They were simply going through the world the best they could.

The women, to the best of my knowledge, were pure and wholesome. They lived and laughed and loved and married and brought up children on this pittance they got from the mills.

A dollar then had greater value than now. I did a lot of shopping for mother and I remember that round steak was twelve cents a pound. Sirloin was fourteen, and short sixteen cents. Rents were low. We had a cottage, ten thousand feet of land, six cherry trees and a pear tree, all for seven dollars a month.

I spoke of the floor in the mill being of North Carolina pine. In the alleys we used to run trucks to carry the yarn. These trucks would tear the floor so from time to time every one of us boys would get splinters, pieces of wood an inch to half an inch in our feet. A spinner would put his jack-knife under the skin and pull. If it came out well and good—if not, we had a festered foot for two or three weeks and nearly all the time some boy was walking on his heels, as he had a splinter in the sole of his festered foot or on the sole because he had a festered heel. Suffer! Many a splinter I had in my feet. No medical advice, no help.

AN IRISH BOY IN AMERICA 31

My good mother would bandage it with linseed meal and after two or three weeks it would come out.

When I was nine years old I witnessed a great tragedy. I saw the burning of the Granite Mill No. 1, where twenty-eight men and women were burned to death. I was in No. 2 across the street on the nineteenth of September, 1874. I saw a puff of smoke coming out of the window and a man descending the fire-escape. The fire was in the mule room and over the mule room was the warp, slashing and drawing-in room. The mill had a peaked roof which covered this particular room. The only way out was a big door which led to the tower. This door was said to have been locked. There was no fire escape. One of the slashers got out from the skylight, threw down a rope and slid down to the third floor and was saved. The neighbors rushed mattresses at each end of the mill and some of the boys and girls rushed to the window, said a prayer and jumped. One of those little boys had been a companion of mine in the mill and was sent over to No. 1 a few days before. He jumped, ran home, told his mother the mill was on fire, and dropped dead. Few escaped from that room.

One woman, a Mrs. Murphy, lost three daughters. It had been her custom to bring their breakfast every morning, but that morning of the fire she was in Providence. After the fire for some time she would get the breakfast, fill the pails, walk down to the ruined mill and cry hysterically until some friends would take her home again.

The mill gave no compensation to any of the families whose children were lost. Mrs. Murphy's son was given a job running a pair of mules when the mill was rebuilt. A family named O'Keefe brought suit against the mill. Ben Butler was the lawyer for them, but the mill won. O'Keefe occupied a desirable mill cottage and he was ordered out because he brought suit.

I saw other mills burn down, but mostly at night. Spectacular fires they were, as the pine was all saturated with oil. Then some wise mind made automatic sprinklers to equip the mills so that the heat when it reached one hundred and fifty or one hundred and seventy-five degrees would melt the lead which let the water free. From that day to this there has not been a mill fire until Liggett of the Liggett Stores bought the Pocasset mills. He was not successful and they thought they would dismantle the machinery so that they would not have to pay taxes. These mills were adjoining the main street. In moving the machinery they tore down the sprinklers and the mills got on fire, and Fall River had the worst fire in its history. I think the damage was about ten million dollars.

I went through many strikes and lockouts which Fall River suffered for years and years. I never knew the employees to win a strike. The time seemed always selected by the manufacturers. Once a strike lasted twenty-six weeks. People had no money, they paid no rent, no bills, and as it was in the summer they lived on huckleberries and fished and dug clams, but during that long strike many of the old families were seen to go over the bridge with their little household effects.

Many of the English and Irish left Fall River, and the French Canadians came after them. A fine lot of people they were too. They built many churches, and fine houses; they were fine, wonderful men and women. The only labor organization worth while was the mule spinners' union. They fought all the labor battles. When they went on strike the mills closed. There were no strike breakers because it took a great many years to be able to spin. A boy would be at least a dozen years in the mule room before he became a spinner. The pay was by piece work. If the cotton was good, they made about eleven dollars a week. They resisted every reduction, but after a strike of a month or two went back beaten. When their funds were exhausted a Boston grocery store, Cobb, Bates and Yerxa with a branch store in Fall River would trust them with $10,000 worth of goods. To the credit of the spinners they always paid this amount back in monthly payments and those who could pay cash traded with this firm.

Then the manufacturers got a bright idea. They would throw out the mules, put in spinning frames run by girls, and this was done. So the mule spinner is almost as rare as the bar tender during prohibition. The ring spinners, who were girls, had doffers who were worse than the spinners. All the manufacturers could get out of the doffer was—"Me want more pay."

I don't know just what the nationality of the mill operators in Fall River is today, but I know a doctor on Main Street who ran a drug store and who used to give his service free because he could send them downstairs to his drug store to buy what he advised. When he found it necessary to go away for a few days he left a notice which was printed in fourteen different languages.

When I was a boy the law was that a child under fourteen years of age should go to school three months of the year. From the time I was seven until I was fourteen I got six or nine months schooling. The inspector from the state, who would visit the mill, would be let in at the door by the various overseers, conducted through the departments to see who the children were and if they had school cards. Just before he came in the mule room we were put on an elevator and brought up to the next room, so the inspector when he came through would find one-half or one-quarter of the children and they had school cards; when he went to some other room we came down in the elevators, good for another nine months without going to school.

CHAPTER II

I didn't like the mill and I could see that there was no way to get out of it without an education. At the age of ten I presented myself at the evening school. All the big boys got into the room and into their seats and at that there were more left in the dressing room. Miss Susan B. Wixson was the principal, and she told the rest of the boys that that was all for the present, and for them to come back next year when the school opened. I held my ground, and she said, "Little boy, don't you hear what I say?" But I said, "There's a seat over there." She told me that the boy wasn't there that night, but was coming the next night. I said, "Let me sit there tonight and tomorrow night some other boy will be absent, and the next night someone else." She said, "You come right over here, little boy, I want you." She often visited my home. When I graduated from the evening high school, she had me appointed teacher, where I taught for three years and afterward a year at the commercial high school. I met her with her sister some twenty-five or thirty years afterwards, and she introduced me to her sister as the wonderful boy the world would hear from.

I used to read many books. Every night, when not at school, I went to the public library and of course in the early days it was fiction. I think I read all the authors that were worth while, but I believe that the Oliver Optic, Alger and Kellogg books helped me a great deal. There was a little lesson in each of their stories that was a great help to me. Then again one of the spinners subscribed for the Boston Transcript and the Brooklyn Eagle, which he passed on to me every day, and I used to read Beecher's Sermons and after memorizing them get all the boys together and preach to them. They thought it was great. Good practice for me! I had a wonderful memory at the time and often went to meetings, following which I would relate to the boys in the mill what was said at the meeting. My mother gave me one of the most fascinating books I have ever read, the Lily of Israel. She brought it from Ireland. We had many books from Ireland, I presume from my grandfather's library.

There is one great passage in this book that has appealed to me more than any other that I have read. Our Lady is following the steps of Her Divine Son when she meets a young man who has been blind from birth. He has met Jesus who has given sight to his eyes. The young man tells the mother of the glories that he sees them for the first time, the trees, the birds and the flowers, and the other things of beauty that God has made that his children might enjoy them and be happy. Every good father wants his children to find happiness and when I meet Him at the end of the day when little children come home I want to tell Him what a wonderful good time I had on the earth where He placed me to work and play. I remember taking this book to school with me and in the geography period slipping it behind the covers of the big book. I was so absorbed in the story that when I was called to recite I was not in the room, but in far off Palestine with the Lily of Israel.

My father and mother, while religious, were not church-goers. When the boys and girls were clothed they didn't have any money left to clothe themselves.

AN IRISH BOY IN AMERICA

I received my first communion about the age of nine and was confirmed at twelve. I remember I had no coat at the time and had to get up early in the morning and borrow my brother's coat. I then taught Sunday School for six years and was elected president of the Christian Doctrine Association. I also joined the St. Vincent de Paul Society. This society looks after the poor, one of the greatest organizations for doing good in the world. The members of the association visit the poor, see that they get good advice, food and clothes, and no record is ever kept of it. We were in the parish of the Sacred Heart from the time we came to Fall River till my marriage, 21 years later.

In my last year of evening high school, the first night I was attracted to a very nice, sweet, wholesome looking girl. I said to myself, "I wonder who in the world she is," but I was busy studying English and arithmetic, and she was busy studying German and something else, so we didn't have a chance to meet until the school was over.

The night we got notice from the Devoll mills that our services would be no longer required as the gingham business had proved a failure, I went down the street with four of my crowd, one of whom went to evening high school. As we passed where this girl worked—she worked all day and four nights a week— she was coming out, and seeing that we were of the evening classes, she said, "Pardon me, but we are planning to present to Mr. Smith, the principal, a gold-headed cane, and wouldn't you like to be a party to it?" I said, "Sure," and she told us that we were each to contribute fifty cents. I handed over my half dollar and got a smile and thank-you. Then she turned to my friend and asked him the same thing. He said he would be in on it too, but said, "I'll owe you the half dollar." I saw her face assume a dismayed look, and promptly said I'd lend it to him. I had exactly forty-nine cents, which I loaned him, and that was all I had in the world at the time, but her smile paid me for it.

Two days afterward when passing by her store, she stepped out ready to go home, and said, "Good evening!" Miss Lynch certainly looked good to me, and I asked, "How about the gold-headed cane?" She explained that while she was the chairman of the committee she had to work that evening, and couldn't attend the presentation. In fact they were up at Mr. Smith's house then. I suggested that we walk up to his house and she consented. The party was over when we got there, so we continued our walk. Then we met nearly every night for almost five years, when we were married. I was twenty-eight, and Mary twenty-four. Then the children came, and we moved to Providence, New York, Cleveland, Pittsburgh, Chicago and Boston, and then thirty years later a nice little old lady came into my office and told me that she was Mrs. Smith, the widow of the principal to whom we gave the cane. She said that I was the most worthy of all to have that cherished cane. I prize it for its associations, and it marks the date that Mary and I first walked together, March 19, 1889.

The mill boy of fifty years ago had his hours of play much as a boy of today. In the summer we played marbles, tops and baseball. The great game was Peggy, which I have not seen anyone play for thirty years. The Peggy was about four inches of broom stick whittled to a lead pencil point on each end. The game was to strike one end, make the Peggy rise in the air three or four feet, and hit it with a stick, then the player would appraise the distance that his opponent could jump and so give him twenty or thirty as the case might be. If the opponent was not willing to consider this, he had the privilege of jumping the distance. If he jumped it in the number asked for, the one who hit it got nothing, but if he did not, the number he asked for was added to his score. This developed a lot of fine jumpers, gave us an estimate of distance, and trained the eye as the ball player is trained to hit the ball.

I was pretty good at Peggy, but poor at baseball. I could hit and run, but my hands were too small and too soft to catch the ball. Marbles—I kept the other boys poor. They had to do the buying. We played tag and leap frog and other games that kept us out in the open. These permitted our bodies to develop. In the winter time there was skating and sliding, but few of us had the necessary clothing to go out in the open of a cold day and we had to hug the stove.

Many of the boys and girls, owing to insufficiency of food and neglected colds, passed away with tuberculosis. In those days there were no rubbers. There were high boots, and after being exposed to the snow they would shrink several sizes during the night, with the result in the morning the members of the family would go around the kitchen pulling on the boots and kicking the baseboard until they got the boots on. Many of the winters when I was seven, eight and nine, I would go down to the machine shop, get on my father's back and he would carry me the quarter of a mile to our house.

While I was friendly with everyone, for many years I had no chum. I took long walks, read a great deal and in the summer time explored every foot of the woods. Snakes and bugs at that time meant nothing to me. I would go through the woods barefoot, but now if a June bug should come into the house the whole family has to stop everything and capture it before I have any comfort.

I attended about everything that was free, such as political meetings and religious meetings. I heard many wonderful sermons, many great preachers, and among them I enjoyed the great Wendell Phillips, who is said to be the greatest orator of his age.

When I was seventeen the Dominican Missionaries, headed by the great Father McKenna, who afterward became general of this famous order of preachers, gave a mission in our church. I went to confession to him. He asked me to promise to pray for him every day and he would pray for me. When I was thirty-seven I met him again in Fall River, called his attention to the compact we had made and told him I had not failed a single day in remembering him in my prayers. He asked how I was and I told him I was being troubled with ulcers of the eye, so he took me to his hotel and rubbed the eye with a relic of St. Dominic. My eyes were cured shortly afterward.

I prayed for this good man every day until I was fifty-four, when I heard he had been called to his reward, his two hands overflowing with good deeds to lay at the feet of his Creator; then I prayed for his soul from that day until this. Not that he needed them, but that he might pour them into the lap of Our Lady to be applied on the debt some other poor soul has incurred for his transgressions. I have often said that some good saints have been praying for me, else I would never have escaped the dangers that have threatened me.

My mother had a lovely sister who lived in Boston. She would write from time to time and in every letter was something to help us along. She was a maid for many years with the Appletons, a noted Boston family, and with Mrs. Paran Stevens, known all over the country. She used to come to see us about every year and I grew very fond of her and she of me. She had some cataracts form on her eyes, and I went with her to the famous eye specialist, Dr. Derby of Boston. He operated on her in Boston and after many weeks I called for her at the hospital and went with her, eyes still bandaged, to his office for examination. It was a dramatic moment. We both waited in great suspense until the doctor removed the bandages, examined the eyes, and said she would never see again. I brought her home to our house in Fall River, but she never recovered from the shock and a little while after we folded her hands across her breast and laid her away.

I think this gave me a very serious view of life. Then I found a chum, a scholarly boy, the bookkeeper in a wholesale grocery house. We were together every night for nearly seven years. We walked and talked and talked and walked and discussed most every subject that young men of our age discussed. In the seven years I never heard one single immodest word from my chum. His mind was pure as the clear water of a spring. He had an obsession that he would die before he was thirty. All his brothers had died before that age. He would never marry but just wait until he got about thirty and resignedly go to the grave. How I used to josh him and tell him he would marry and have children. He was not prepossessing in appearance and there was something the matter with his arm from childbirth. I never asked him what it was, but the shoulder dropped some three or four inches. My tailor asked me what in the name of God happened to my shoulder because it sympathetically dropped the same three or four inches.

Men who associate together I find think and talk

and walk alike. I believe that environment is a great shaper of destiny. It is the picture we see, the book we read and the men and women we associate with that makes or breaks us. This chum of mine up to the time I met the girl who is now my wife, never had a girl nor had I. We never visited anywhere where there were girls except once we brought him up to a bakery which I used to frequent in my younger days. There were four fine, sweet handsome girls there, all sisters. I was very friendly with the two boys who did the baking, but the father who ran the business never seemed to look on me with favor.

Tim McCarthy, my chum, who wasn't going to marry, was quite positive on this point until a nice, lovely red-haired school teacher with a come-hither look in her eye smiled at Tim and they married and she gave him eight beautiful children. He has gone to his reward, and looking back after a long life I say that he had a splendid character and I believe that there were very few sins that he would have to do penance for.

In the seven years I went with him I never saw him spend a cent. I would buy a couple of apples, peanuts or a newspaper, for which he would scold me and would ask me where I would be when I was thirty if I squandered my money. I laughed and said I would be a great man some day and have lots of money.

But my great companion was my mother. She sat up every night until her seven boys were in. They would come in, salute her and go up to their rooms. But I would always sit by the side of the fire and discuss the events of the day. I was seldom out after nine o'clock except when I went to night school and then it would not be much later than nine-thirty. The only heat in the house was in the kitchen and all of us boys in the winter would take off our hats and coats and shoes in the kitchen and go up to the "refrigerator." It surely was cold in that attic, but we slept three in a bed so that we could keep one another warm. I got in the habit of saying my prayers in the kitchen and a thousand times or more my good mother would take me off my knees when I was fast asleep and send me up to bed. After I was married I used to go to see her once a week and sit and chat with her about the way the world was going.

Mother's room was off the kitchen and she had a feather bed which was brought from Ireland. The rest of us had straw beds, but anyone who got sick would go down to mother's bed and father would go to the attic. This gave her a chance to nurse the patient. My brother John had typhoid fever, and day and night he was nursed for seven weeks. The only boyhood illness I ever remember was when I was twenty-four. I had the measles—that was the night the Fall River City Hall burned down. I could see the flames but they would not let me leave the bed. When mother was sick unto death, we had no money for nurses so the family conclave decided that the girls would nurse during the day and the boys at night. Jim on Sunday night, Tom, Monday night and I Tuesday, Joe Wednesday, and so on. Mother for some reason was moved into the room opposite the parlor when my night came. I was there at the time agreed, shortly after nine o'clock. My sisters went to bed and I sat on the sofa in the parlor opposite the bedroom so I could watch the patient and answer her calls. I had worked hard and long all day and then I had taught school, and I was pretty tired, but I sat there as faithfully as any sentinel in the army. Nature asserted itself and I fell asleep, leaving my mother untended.

When I woke after a deep sleep I found my head in my mother's lap. She found me asleep, got out of bed, put my head in her lap and she and my guardian angel watched over me. She died a few days after, and seven of us boys marched after the hearse to the cemetery. At the time it was a custom for the bearers to fill the grave. When the stones from the first shovel struck my mother's coffin, I thought it was the most terrible thing that had come to me in my whole life.

CHAPTER III

The mill exacted much from me, but it taught me much that was helpful in after life, respect for superiors, carrying out orders promptly and efficiently, how to get along with my fellow workers and win and hold their respect, how to cut out waste motion and make every movement count. Long before I read Taylor and Emerson I was a student of efficiency. I always looked for the shortest method of doing an act. When I had been with Julius Mathews a few years, he said one day, "Dave, I didn't see you in the Holy Name Parade Sunday. I looked for you." "Mr. Mathews," I replied, "there were 45,000 men in the parade, surely you did not see every man in the parade." "No, Dave," he said, "knowing you as I do, I knew you would find an easy way, so I looked only for the men on horseback."

About a week after I left the mill, I saw an ad in a newspaper for a young man wanted to learn the newspaper business. I got the place, and while forty-five years in it I have not learned it yet. The manager of the newspaper, which had just started in Fall River, was named McGill. He was the son of a minister. A fine handsome chap, six feet two, and wore a silk topper so that he was some sight. He explained to me I would have to solicit subscriptions for this newspaper, the Fall River Tribune, a morning newspaper. My job was to get subscriptions for this paper at six dollars per year. I asked him why people would pay six dollars a year for what they could buy at two cents a copy; he said they would do it, though I could not see it, but was willing to give it a try. I explained to Mr. McGill that I was a mill boy and had not been out in the world, and asked him to let me start in Somerset, some five miles away, where they didn't know me. I would then get my nerve up and start in Fall River.

I started the following morning, Friday; I came down at eight-thirty to take the train for Somerset, and Mr. McGill called to know what was the matter with me, for he said that I was late. I explained that you could not see people at seven o'clock in the morning, for they have to get their breakfasts and get the children out to school. But he knew different, so I agreed the following morning to go out at seven o'clock. Then he asked if I could get ads or hold down the telegraph editor's desk. I said sure I could hold the telegraph editor's desk by sitting on it; that was the only way I thought I could do it. He said that if I could get ads he would give me twenty-five per cent commission. He thought I could find one somewhere for the Tribune. I asked him when I would get my money and he said when I brought in the contract. I then asked him to give me the eight dollars a week that he agreed to pay me for getting subscriptions, but he refused; he said he could not afford it.

I came back in an hour with a ten-dollar contract. They gave me my two dollars and a half, and the next morning it was a twenty-dollar contract and they had to give me five dollars. I don't remember now what happened Monday, but Tuesday I brought in an order from C. T. Shearer for one hundred and sixty dollars, and forty dollars was due me. They found Shearer and asked about it, and he said he heard my talk on the Tribune and decided to use it. They didn't have the cash to give me my forty dollars, but it was decided to give me an order at Shearer's, so I bought myself some clothes and thus took my commission.

This worked so well that the next day I said to my mother, "Could you use some furniture?" and upon her assent proceeded to make a contract with N. P. Berard and asked that I receive my commission in an order on Berard's, so he was quite pleased to think that I used twenty-five per cent of his contract. We got a parlor stove, couch and half a dozen chairs. Furniture in those days was sold at five and ten cent store prices. Every day I would bring in an advertisement. At the end of three weeks I met McGill and he said, "I have sad news for you; I have been discharged as manager, and if you must know why, it is because I hired you. You will be discharged when you get to the office." "Well," I said, "what is the matter with these men?" It seemed that they thought I was making all the money, upon which I replied that they got seventy-five per cent and all repeats and I got a quarter of it and no repeats. He said, "You are right, but for being a good man you are going to be fired in the morning." I cut my visit to the office that day, and in the morning the new manager greeted me and said he was sorry, but he had orders to discharge me and combine the two jobs. He then confided to me that he was a good manager, but he hated getting ads. They didn't get any for four or five months, and they went out of business.

My brother, who was a director on the Herald, got them to employ me at eight dollars per week. I found I was to be a reporter in the morning and an advertising man in the afternoon, because no paper could support a man on advertising. The first job given me was longshore reporting. I was to take a five-mile walk along the wharves and get news of the ships going in and out. I started bravely and after the first mile came to the lumber yard of A. Homer Skinner. He was on the water front, and I went in to get shipping news. Old man Skinner was playing checkers. I watched and he said, "Do you play?" I told him I did, and so we played and I beat him two games. He wanted the third, but I said I had to go about my business. He said, "Listen boy, I'm a correspondent on the Boston Advertiser, and all these ship captains know me and come here on their arrival. If you stick around and play with me, I will give you all the news I have." I played checkers with him. I brought in the news to the editor and he said they had never received so much. Every morning I would play checkers at Skinner's, and come back with a bag of news. We got very fond of each other. Skinner was one of the Forty-niners who went to California. I wrote the story of his life, which was printed in the Herald, and our paper had the finest shipping news of any in the city.

As a reward for my fine work I was assigned to the police courts, and for five years I covered every phase of court reporting. We had the district court, probate court and superior court. We had everything from ordinary drunkenness to murder. It was while I was court reporter that what was known as the famous Lizzie Borden murder case came up, and I reported the preliminaries. This was the case where a father and mother were found dead in their home about eleven o'clock one August morning in 1892. The father was the richest man in Fall River and known to be very miserly. Lizzie Borden was arrested and arraigned for the murder of her father and step-mother, and she was discharged after a trial that lasted a long time. Nearly the whole town believed her guilty, but a jury of good men acquitted her after deliberating for an hour and six minutes.

At the end of five years court reporting, I asked the editor to take me away from the job or I would go crazy. There was so much sin and suffering that I could not stand it. It was in this court I saw the great evil committed by the saloons. Most of the cases were for drunkenness, and I have seen so many mothers pay fines for drunken husbands and children that I decided the saloon was the greatest evil this country had. That was forty years ago; I am just as firmly convinced now that the saloon has done more injury to the people in this country than any other known agency. They not only robbed their customers, but they drove them mad, so that they sent them home to abuse their wives and children. I have seen it not only in the courts, not only in my neighborhood, but nearer home than that.

About that time Hearst and his papers were running a series of cartoons by Davenport about the evils of the saloon. I remember taking this page with a cartoon on it and writing, "God bless you, Mr. Hearst." The one great redeeming feature of the Hearst newspapers was their fight against whiskey. They would not take a whiskey advertisement. Brisbane wrote for years on the curse of whiskey. The depression like politics makes strange bedfellows. Now all the Hearst papers carry whiskey advertising, and Brisbane's great pen never touches on the subject.

The advertising on the Herald began to grow. When I first solicited advertising merchants used to laugh, but the second, third, fourth, or fifth time they would listen. All advertising was sold on yearly contracts for once a week or twice or three times a week for a year. I remember meeting one of the boys in the mill. He asked me what I was doing, and I told him soliciting advertising for the Herald. He said, "What are you going to do when you get all of it?" I told him I assumed it would be some days before I could get all of it.

I was so successful they increased my pay to nine dollars, then ten dollars. Finally, after five or six years, I got thirteen dollars a week. The managing owner was Mr. James E. O'Connor, who was clerk in the Devoll mills when I worked there. He married the daughter of a rich wholesaler in liquor and bought controlling interest in the Herald. One day he asked me out for a drive and congratulated me on my work. He said that he was leaving the Herald as manager and by all rights I was entitled to the job, but he thought it best for a real American to be manager, so he had secured the services of Mr. George Buffington, but Mr. Buffington had taken it with the proviso that I be kept on the job. "Now," Mr. O'Connor said, "I'll give you at the end of the year a purse of money far greater than any raise of pay will amount to."

I applied for Buffington's job as manager of the Globe, and I thought I would get it. I thought my record entitled me to it. The Globe was then owned and controlled by a group of men who were all Irish. The big owner was Quinlan Leary, a wholesale liquor dealer; next was his cousin, C. S. Greene, the piano dealer, John W. Cummings, a great lawyer, D. D. Sullivan, an undertaker.

These men mentioned as directors in the Globe had a strangle hold in the city. If you wanted to live in peace and comfort, you had to patronize them. They made Cummings mayor of Fall River and at that time the mayor gave out the licenses, so unless you bought your beer from Quinlan Leary, there was nothing doing. They made Sullivan postmaster of the city of

Fall River and they were so powerful that you had to play with them or you couldn't play. They had tried to get control of the Herald, but my brother had fought them successfully, with the result that they didn't like me. C. S. Greene made two or three propositions to me, and finally said, "Listen, Dave, you are never going to get anything where you are; get into my business and be my advertising manager and I will give you a dollar more than they are paying you." I was married then. The Herald had given me an extra dollar and we found we could get along fine on fourteen dollars a week. The trouble was we didn't always get the money. Many a time Buffington said he didn't have the money and would I take an order for merchandise. I think this led me to take Greene's offer, so I became his advertising manager. I found that advertising was only one per cent of his business, and I went from door to door ringing bells, and was quite successful as a salesman. I got very fond of Mr. Greene. He was the finest gentleman in Fall River. He had fought in the army and navy both, but he never paraded with the G. A. R.

He was very unassuming, well groomed and very spiritual. Many a time we went out together while he visited various poor families. What happened there I don't know, but he always stopped at the corner grocery and had a basket with provisions sent to these homes, always warning me to say nothing about it. He was offered the mayoralty nomination many times, but always refused it. While I left him, our friendship continued for the seven years that I remained in Fall River. I found when I went to Greene's that I had to work four evenings a week, three to nine and one to eleven o'clock. In the newspaper business we quit at five, so I decided I would not be a piano man. I told him at the end of a year I would like to go on to the Globe. He said there was no chance. They didn't want me. Well, I said I was going to go anyhow, and now that night school was beginning I would like to leave because if I left two months later I would not have a school.

Then he told me that the reason they had not given me the job on the Globe was because the directors felt that this paper, run by Irishmen, should have an American as manager.

The new manager, a newspaper man from Lowell, resigned after holding the position a year.

In the meantime, five of the Globe directors purchased a paper in New Bedford for $25,000. They told Mr. Greene that they wanted me for business manager. Mr. Greene told them that I was going to stay with him. These five men ran the New Bedford daily until they lost $50,000 and then closed it up.

A few days after I left Mr. Greene, he asked me to manage his business for a few weeks as he was going to the Atlanta Exposition, and asked what I would charge him for the two weeks. I explained it meant leaving night school, so I would charge him twenty dollars. This was fine.

The next day he said I would not have to give up night school, that his wife would take care of the store in the evening, so what would I charge then. I looked him right in the eye and said twenty dollars. I managed the store for the two weeks. I did considerable advertising and the Lord was kind to me, for while the average piano sale was one a week, I sold seven pianos in two weeks and also two organs. Mr. Greene said he wished he had stayed away a month. I collected my money and thought he would make me an offer to come back to the business. I was working on my brother's paper, The Catholic Advocate, and while he didn't know it, all I was earning was ten dollars a week, plus four dollars night school work, which was not much to support a home and pay for furniture bought on the installment plan.

Mr. Greene walked home with me a day or two afterwards, and said he wanted me back as manager, that he felt he would not be long in the business. I told him he would stay in it until he was carried out and this came to pass. I told him Mary was expecting a baby and if he would give me twenty dollars a week I would come back. I did not know then that there was a gentleman's agreement among the Main Street merchants that no salesman was worth more than twelve dollars a week. Greene violated this agreement when he gave me fifteen dollars, but he would not pay the twenty dollars a week. He said, "Dave, you ought to be in business for yourself; go into the sewing machine business, hire a store, get men and machines and send the bills to me; I will pay them all and set you on your feet." I refused and he said then that he would put me on the Globe.

The new manager of the Globe was C. F. Kelly, a high school graduate with a year in a commercial college. They paid him twelve dollars a week. The directors found that some advertisers were only paying twenty-five per cent of the rates, so they increased the rates and ordered that all advertisers pay the new rate. Mr. Kelly's first call was on Bailey, the installment dealer, and when he stated his errand, which was increasing Bailey's rate five times the old rate, Mr. Bailey said, "Young man, what is your name and how long have you been on the job?" Kelly told him, and Mr. Bailey said, "Get to hell out of here and don't come back until you get more sense." All the advertisers followed Bailey's decree and the Globe was minus a great deal of advertising. So they appointed me as advertising solicitor at eighteen dollars per week and they raised Kelly's pay to twenty dollars, for he was the manager. When I got twenty dollars, they gave him twenty-five, and when they gave me twenty-two dollars, they gave him thirty dollars, but our earnings were about the same as I wrote advertising outside.

In a month or two I had all the advertisers back paying the increased rate.

One of my advertisers built the Hudner building and said to write it up for the papers, for which he would pay ten dollars. I said, "Michael, the Globe will not publish a line of it." The Herald and News printed my two-column story, but the Globe, which carried a large advertising contract from Hudner, did not print a line.

Mr. Greene called up the editor, and asked why Hudner's story did not appear in the Globe. The editor said he had seven reporters and the services of all of them were at Mr. Hudner's disposal. Greene said, "Say, Kennedy, none of your men can write like Dave; you run that story tomorrow." It ran.

I wrote Mr. Greene's advertisements for seven years. Five years afterwards, when in Boston, George Gallup of the Cosmopolitan magazine looked me up. He told me he had an order for five full pages in his magazine from Mr. Byrnes, advertising manager of the Chickering Piano Company. Copy was prepared in New York and was rejected by Mr. Byrnes as hopeless, and he cancelled the order.

A five-page cancellation to a magazine man is like an order to be shot at sunrise. So Gallup asked if there was a man in Boston who could write an advertisement that would be acceptable. Mr. Byrnes said there was a man named David S. Lawlor whom he knew could do it. He had only met him once and seen one piece of his copy, but it was beautiful. If Gallup could get me to write it he felt it would be acceptable.

Gallup found me and offered me fifty dollars to write the advertisement. It was then Friday and the magazine closed Tuesday. Monday I met Gallup at Chickering's and gave him the copy. Byrnes said it was superb, so I got the fifty dollars and George Gallup was a happy man. He gave me a cigar, took me to lunch, and became one of my best friends.

CHAPTER IV

I was very anxious to succeed on the Globe. Every day I used to purchase the New York papers to see what was doing in that great city to show to my advertisers and inspire them to do greater things in advertising. One day I brought to Charlie Gaudette, the second best jeweler in town, a page out of the New York Journal. It was a magnificent advertisement. There was a great circle in the center of the page, and this circle was filled with all kinds of jewelry. The top corner of the advertisement was the picture of a lady with a lorgnette peering down at what was in the circle. It was an advertisement of Lambert Brothers, a great New York jewelry house of thirty years ago. I laid it down, and said, "Charlie, why don't you run an ad like that?" He said, "Where will I get the cuts, it would cost a fortune, and I haven't one-half of those things in my store." "Well," I said to him, "put in what you have." Then we got a Keystone Jewelry catalogue, cut out the pictures of what Charlie did carry, and pasted them in the illustration. Wherever it said Lambert we drew in Gaudette; then we found a picture of Santa Claus with a pack on his back and placed this over the lady, so the steal would not be so apparent. I took this copy to Providence, as I had met the engraver there who had told me about the halftones which were just coming into use in newspapers. He looked at the advertisement and shook his head regretfully. He explained that the biggest plate they could make was one-half a page, so this could not

AN IRISH BOY IN AMERICA 57

be produced. "Well," I said, "Ferguson, two half pages make a whole page." He agreed with me. When the proofs were submitted to Gaudette, we had to read them through a looking glass because they were reversed, but we got the two plates and Charlie Gaudette gave me an order for seventy-seven dollars. That would be fifty cents an inch. It surely did look good. Gaudette said a hundred people came in and wanted to know if he had purchased the Globe. He had never done so much business before. Gifford, the leading jeweler, who ran about five inches, told me confidentially that Gaudette was a damn liar, that he didn't have half the stuff he advertised in his store. It was my thought to take all the New York papers and offer to make the cuts for the advertisers, but the directors of the Globe decided that they would not do it. They did utter a shriek at the bill for the plate, which was twenty dollars.

During my seven years on the Globe, I went to Boston every Tuesday, looking for business, and I got a lot of advertising. Pettengill and Company were the great agency at that time rivalling the well-known firm of N. W. Ayer. From the Pettengill agency came Dr. Greene's Nervura, Lydia Pinkham, Regal Shoe, Chase & Sanborn and hundreds of other accounts. The space buyer was a German named Holfelder. We became very intimate and I found him one of the most conscientious men that I have ever met. He had a partnership arrangement with Pettengill and the firm held that money was not due to the publisher until the firm was billed for advertising. The publishers were very lax in billing and in those days thousands of dollars worth of advertising was never billed. Holfelder maintained the money was due the paper. A disagreement arose over this question, and he retired from the firm and occupied the position of space buyer. He was a wonderful man. Many of the special representatives who knew all the space buyers in the country at that period told me that they have never found the equal of Mr. Holfelder.

He seemed troubled one day, and I asked him what the matter was. He said he had a very religious mother and he had married against her advice a woman who was not of his faith, and their only child had been brought up in the wife's religion, so he was sorrowful, for after his death and when his soul was in purgatory he would have no one to pray for him. I promised that I would pray for him after his death, a promise I have kept daily for more than twenty-five years.

His assistant was Frank Allen, one of the handsomest men I ever met in my life. Cheerful, wholesome, really talented, a wonderful singer and all round good fellow, maybe too good a fellow. He asked Holfelder one day why it was that all business went to Fall River; whether it was high quality or cheap, it always went to Dave Lawlor. Mr. Holfelder only smiled and said that Dave Lawlor said the Globe was a great medium and he believed him.

I got to know Mr. Pettengill very intimately some ten or fifteen years after the failure of his great advertising agency, and he said that the failure was mostly due to buying Greene's Nervura for $500,000. This took a lot of cash and then he had given the Lydia Pinkham account to Mr. Wetherald to look after and when the business grew so that this company was spending $500,000 yearly with Pettengill, Wetherald threatened to take the account away unless he accepted five per cent commission instead of fifteen per cent. This was accepted by Mr. Pettengill and he found that he could not place the business for the five per cent. I found Mr. Pettengill to be a delightful old gentleman.

I was able to do some business for him later, writing copy, etc., and I found him a real intelligent, God-fearing man. He told me when he was celebrating the twenty-fifth anniversary of his business that those in charge of the celebration sent invitations to every newspaper, magazine and every special representative in the country. As his was a big agency, nearly all of them responded with a gift. Those in the papers in the bigger cities vied with each other in the expensiveness of the gift which they sent. The presents aggregated sixty or seventy thousand dollars, and shortly afterward they were put in storage with all his furniture. His only child died, and Mr. and Mrs. Pettengill lived at a hotel in the Back Bay. He said he paid $20,000 in storage charges where those gifts and the furniture were stored and the best offer he could get was $10,000 from a second hand furniture company in Boston, so the publisher's gifts to Pettengill are now scattered in many homes throughout greater Boston.

I used to visit the newspaper offices to see how things were being done on a big scale, so I got to know Mr. Haskell of the Herald, Taylor of the Globe, and W. A. Grozier of the Post. Once I asked Mr. Grozier for a job on his advertising staff. He asked me why I selected the Post, and I told him they didn't have any business. And this was true. Those were the days when Mr. Marchant, now advertising director of the Post, was foreman of the composing room. Marchant would sell the old cuts and old metal and get money to buy the new type. Marchant improved the Lanston typesetting machine and the linotype machine, and when offered a compensation said that he would rather have them give Mr. Grozier a reduction in the price of the machines which he had purchased. E. A. Grozier remembered this loyalty of Marchant, and made him advertising director some twenty years ago. In 1929 the Post carried a trifle over sixteen million lines of advertisements, which brought in about seven million dollars.

I met Mr. E. A. Grozier many times afterward in soliciting for Printers Ink. He was then a semi-invalid, and used to sit bundled up in a shawl. He had a marvelous mind. One of the best stories I ever heard about him was told me by the publisher of the Boston Journal, a rival morning newspaper. Munsey had bought the Journal and lost half a million in trying to get the Post's circulation, and he sold it for a song. Greene lost a quarter of a million, passed it on to Hale and his losses were over $300,000. Then Ware took it and lost his money, and his friends' money, and one day Ware found it would be impossible for him to meet the payroll. Looking across the street at the Post, he thought if Grozier were there he would go and ask him for the loan, but Grozier was at home ill.

Acting on the impulse of the moment, he telephoned Grozier's house for an appointment. When Ware got there, the sick man greeted him, passed him some cigars, and asked him what was on his mind. Ware stated that he could not meet his payroll of $2800. Mr. Grozier said, "If you can't meet it this week, how about next week?" Well, he didn't know, but thought that there might be a chance if he could get by this week. Mr. Grozier said, "Ware, I won't give you one week's payroll which you say is $2800, but I will give you four or five weeks' payroll," and had his secretary make out a check to Mr. Ware for $15,000. Ware said, with tears in his eyes, "I don't know whether you will ever get it back." Grozier said, "I don't want it back, but if the time comes when you are able to pay it back, look up some struggling young publisher and give it to him."

On these trips to Boston I made plans often to see Hood or Everett of Hood's Sarsaparilla or Pullen, who was advertising manager of Ayer's Cherry Pectoral, and then Thompson of Moxie, by going to Lowell. Hood was a great advertiser of his famous sarsaparilla, made considerable money and invested it in Jersey cows. Ayer spent more money than Hood, made far more money and invested it in the mills of Lawrence, and it was his daughter who married William I. Wood, who became President of the American Woolen Company.

The sarsaparillas have been gone for years, but Moxie still remains. They have had quite a business here in New England and they have just organized a national company. In Fall River we had a drink which tasted very much like Moxie, called Francis' Tonic. I mentioned the similarity to Mr. Burr, the son-in-law of Francis, and he said that they were both made from the same formula.

Thompson advertised and got a wonderful business. Francis did not advertise and his tonic has long ago been thrown into the discard. I have found in many cases it is the man who makes the proposition rather than the proposition makes the man. If Thompson had had Francis Tonic and Francis, Moxie, then Moxie would now be dead and Francis Tonic the great seller.

A train used to leave Lowell every afternoon for the Fall River line boat. Coming home one afternoon on this train, I was invited by a gentleman apparently seventy-five or eighty, to play whist. After three or four hands he smiled at me and said, "You play a wonderful game of whist, young man." I replied, "Yes, but in you I recognize a master." He said there was no excuse for his not being a good player, as his son is champion of Canada, his daughter champion of Massachusetts, and the Great Hamilton a visitor at his house nearly every night, but he wondered where I learned the game. At the end of the run I explained to him that I used to go up from Fall River to Boston and sit in and watch whist games, these men being daily commuters, one of them being D. M. Anthony, a very rich man from Fall River who was interested in the Swift Company of Chicago. I was invited to be his partner one day and he abused my playing all the way to Boston.

He was what is popularly known as a crab. I didn't sit with him on the way back, but I went to the library before I went home and got Hamilton's book (600 pages) on whist. I studied this every night for a month, first hand, second hand, third hand, fourth hand, then I organized a group of Holy Name boys and taught them how to play whist as taught by this great master. After six months I hung around Anthony's seat and waited to be invited into the game. The first hand that was played I trumped in on a doubtful trick and Mr. Anthony began to scold me. The other players looked at me with a great deal of sympathy, knowing that I was due for a good dose of medicine. I said to him, "Mr. Anthony, you have been playing the game for a long time, but just what is your authority for saying I was wrong? Hamilton is supposed to be the greatest master on whist and what I did was according to his teachings. Cavendish says in his book the same thing, and now, Mr. Anthony, just what is your authority?"

I thought he would have a stroke, and the other players said, "Anthony, at last you have met your master." Anthony never afterward questioned my ability. I could play any card any way and it was all right with him. He later told me this story: For his second wife he had taken a model employed by the R. H. White Company. Shortly after the marriage she invited many of the shop girls to her home in Fall River to meet her husband. After the dinner there was a whist game. And Mr. Anthony drew for a partner a lovely young girl. Her plays didn't suit him and he scolded her several times. She opened her big blue eyes and looked at him and finally she made a play that was terrible and Anthony said to her, "Madam, I thought you told me you played whist." The girl laid down her cards, and said, "Yes, I play whist, but, you old fool, I don't work at it." A lot of us work at our games instead of playing at them.

Mr. Anthony told me that it was his money, brains and courage that made the great Swift business in Chicago. When he met Swift he was a Cape Cod butcher. Anthony got the patents on the refrigerator car, raised the money for the Chicago enterprise, and it was his plans that were carried out and made this company such a great company. He was in charge of the estate of Swift for a great many years, and that is what brought him back and forth to Boston every day for more than fifty years. He said that a man in Fall River had been very kind to him and put him on his feet financially, and he hoped this man would fall overboard so that he could, at the risk of his own life, jump overboard and save the life of one who had been so kind to him, but he never thought to pass that kindness on.

In the seven years that I went to Boston I noticed one very peculiar thing about this rich man. He never bought a paper. When the train arrived in Taunton he would stop the game, look around, say, "Pardon me, gentlemen," and pick up a paper or two left by those who had left the train. That was not once or twice, but every day. I told my brother about this when we were in the West together. He said it was impossible. I said, "All right, some day you will see." Then afterward, coming up to Boston together, we sat in a car watching Mr. Anthony and his partners play. When the train got to Taunton, he looked around, said "Pardon me" and picked up a paper. My brother said, "I'll be damned!"

CHAPTER V

In Fall River my last year of school teaching was in the commercial school called Shumaker and Clark's. I got very friendly with those two gentlemen. I used to solicit their advertising, which amounted to very little. It was in that school I delivered my first advertising talk shortly after I was married. Clark used to question me on advertising, and said to me one day, "I feel some day I will get to be one of the biggest advertisers in this country." I said, "What you feel is rheumatism." But he did become one of the big advertisers. It happened this way: A hypnotist came to the city under the name of Sage. Now his real name was Neil, and he was the son of a minister in Kansas. They had been in school together and were intimate friends. Neil dabbled in hypnotism and to save the good name of his father he adopted the name of Sage. Sage came over to the school to meet his friend Clark, and met Shumaker. Shumaker's two boys were present at the interview, and the actions of the younger led Sage to say, "Hey, kid, cut out biting your finger nails, that's a bad habit." Mr. Shumaker said he wished Sage could make him stop; he said that he had done everything.

"Huh," said Sage, "I'll stop him." He sat him in the chair, hypnotized him and inhibited him so that he could not raise his hands to bite his finger nails again. He then restored the young man to normal again. The boy raised his hands once or twice half way to his mouth and everybody laughed.

Clark said, "You have a great thing there; why don't you let us put your lessons in book form? I think I could sell them for five dollars apiece." But Sage didn't have the time nor the money.

Clark said, "You will be here a week; we have thirty or forty girls here learning stenography; give dictation to them and we will take care of the rest of it." This was done. They had no money for printing, so the lessons were run off by the janitor from the Neostyle.

The whole cost of the work was eighteen cents. They advertised it in several of the leading papers, offering the lessons for five dollars, giving the address a certain number, Rochester, New York. A couple of weeks afterward Clark got a wire to come on, as there was trouble. He found in Rochester that there had been a great number of five dollar bills sent in. One bookkeeper could not handle the replies, with the result that complaint had been made to the Post Office Department, which contemplated issuing a fraud order. Clark saw the difficulty was in the bookkeeping and promised the government that this would be taken care of in short order and he would have the books sent immediately.

The first year he was given a salary of $10,000. The next year he got $20,000 and then he bought the business from Sage, went to Europe and opened up offices in London, Paris, Berlin and other cities. He told me he had offices in every civilized place in the world except Russia; he could not get into that country and he questioned whether it was civilized. He wired me to come on as his advertising manager, and I refused. I explained the condition of my wife's health at that time would not permit it, but when I was going to Montreal via Niagara Falls we would touch Charlotte, which is six miles from Rochester, and if he cared to see me I would be delighted to see him. It was a terrible night on the trip over from Toronto. The boat was full and the storm terrific.

Clark and his wife and Sage and his wife planned to go to Montreal with us to convince me that Rochester was the place for me. We had only about ten minutes together, for they could not get a stateroom, and I didn't become advertising manager of Clark's. I did visit him several years after on my way to and from Chicago. The second or third time I called on him he had twenty-one offices in the one building, two hundred and twenty stenographers and clerks, and was paying half the postage of the City of Rochester and making half a million a year. I stayed at his house that night and asked him why he didn't do something for Shumaker, who, seeing the success that Clark had made, had written a book on double entry bookkeeping.

Shumaker was a worthwhile fellow. He had been principal of a commercial school in New Jersey, and head bookkeeper for the Baldwin Locomotive Works. He had dictated this work to his stenographer students and had the job run off on the Neostyle as before and advertised them for five dollars in some of the trade papers. The returns were not very good. Shumaker wanted me to sell this whole thing for $1,000 for he needed money very badly, but I could not interest capital to that great amount. Clark sold out his interest and Shumaker's interest in the school and brought him on to Rochester. The year after I met Shumaker he explained to me that his business was but one department of Clark's. Clark kept fifty-one per cent of each line of business and those in charge had forty-nine per cent. "Dave, when I did this business on the Neostyle, it cost me eighteen cents. Clark has had it printed and added pencils and paper so the cost to us is twenty-eight cents. We have advertised it in the daily papers for ten dollars, but on condition that the purchaser pay us an additional twenty dollars when he becomes a double entry bookkeeper. $228,000 was made in the last year." Some years ago I wrote Clark and asked him what became of Shumaker. He said he had made a lot of money and bought some gold and silver mines. He didn't know how much water was in the mines, but he had invested a million or so.

Among the wonderful fellows I have met through my life was Frank Post of the Pettengill Agency. He asked me where I was going one summer, and I said, "My wife and sister are in the hospital with typhoid fever, so I don't think I can go anywhere. Mary is convalescing and I think a trip would do her good, but I don't see how we can go."

He asked, "How would you like a trip to Montreal?" I said, "Great" so the doctor advised Mary to go and we went to Montreal on the day train and saw this great country that lies between Boston and the Canadian border. When we arrived in Montreal I found I had a letter of introduction to the president of the Grand Trunk Railway and one to the president of the Richelieu and Ontario Navigation Company. I presented my letter at the Railway office and a very courteous gentleman explained that Sir John Hay or someone like that was not there, but what could they do for me. I said, "Nothing." He asked me if I would like to see Niagara Falls. This had been one of the great desires of my life, so he wrote out transportation to Niagara Falls and back to Montreal with pullman seats. I never got such a fine reception in my life.

I said to Mary, "Let's see what the fellow on the boat will do." He was very gracious. Didn't I want to see Niagara Falls? I explained that the railroad kindly had fixed this up.

He said, "You don't want to come back on the train, board our boat and come back through the Thousand Islands, shoot the rapids, etc." So we went to Toronto and saw Niagara Falls, had a marvelous trip and shot the rapids. I found also that we were entitled to a trip to Quebec, the Saguenay River, and back to Montreal. Those men in Montreal were really handsome givers. We went to the Shrine of Ste. Anne de Beaupre, visited the cathedrals in Quebec and Montreal and many of the churches and returned home safely, Mary's health being very much better. I might say that she got sick in Toronto. Her face broke out. She looked to me as though she had smallpox, and I could see having to put her in the hospital and getting a job in the Toronto paper until she was cured. I went to see a fine doctor who had just recovered from typhoid himself. He said it wasn't smallpox, but was simply indigestion. She had eaten too freely after her illness and he said she would be all right. That was the night we took the boat and I noticed she was sick and rang the bell for the steward again and again, but no one paid any attention. I was wild, and the only one I could find on the boat was the bartender. He explained that the storm was so terrific that he thought he and I were the only ones on the boat not sick. I wanted to know what to do for my wife. "Give her a tumbler of brandy." I said, "She won't take it." He said, "You're her husband, make her take it." Mary took the brandy and went to sleep and I took what was left and went to sleep, and from that day to this she has enjoyed very good health.

My next trip to Boston I met Post. I said, "Frank, how can I ever square myself with you for this wonderful trip you have given Mary and me?" He said, "Listen, boy, I never keep a debit and credit account of my friends." I thought that was a great saying. Then afterward I was able to do something for him. He has gone along, and I hope he has found his credits many and his debts few.

CHAPTER VI

There was a little five and ten cent store on Main Street run by E. P. Charlton, a nice, wholesome fellow. He opened the store in another city and then another, and in a little while he joined all these stores with Woolworth and became vice president. Charlton died a few years ago, and left $25,000,000. He was when rich the same wholesome, democratic fellow he was when he opened his first store in Fall River.

There was a cloak and suit store opened up by Cherry and Webb, two Canadian boys. They used to have good handbills printed until I convinced them that the Globe would pay them better. These boys now have eight or ten stores. I found the location for them in Providence, in fact made them take it against their will. Ten years afterward Cherry told me that they made $1,000,000 in that one store. "What did we give you, Dave," he asked, "for picking out this store?" "Fifty Dollars," said I. "I feel ashamed," he said. "If you feel that way, I will send Mrs. Lawlor down to pick out a dress." He told me she could have the finest dress in the store. They are doing a great business. Cherry is in the Providence store, Webb the Fall River store, and all the other stores through various managers.

The first real ad I ever sold was to C. T. Shearer. He came to Fall River when he was fifty-two years old, with $1,000. He told me everything he ever tackled was a failure. He opened his little store on the corner of Fourth and Pleasant Streets, fully a quarter of a mile from the business section. He tried to get goods in Boston and they all turned him down with the exception of Mr. Fitzpatrick, the head of Brown, Durrell. In seven or eight years Shearer had built a business of $900,000 a year and then he sold it to a brother of Mr. Fitzpatrick of Brown, Durrell and some other people. He told me that he had leased a store in Worcester and while the store in Fall River was known in Fall River as the rag shop, he wanted to attract a pretty good trade in Worcester. Would I go to Worcester and tell the newspapers what a fine fellow he was and how much advertising he would do, and get notices from these papers—the Telegram, Gazette and the Spy? If I would do these things he would give me twenty-five dollars.

I went to Worcester, got a fine notice in the Gazette and the Spy, but the Telegram explained that they never gave a notice to anyone. I made my report to Mr. Shearer, and he said, "Well, you have done two-thirds of the job very well and I will pay you for two-thirds," and gave me his check for $16.67. He has passed away, but the store in Worcester does a volume of business that runs into millions. I dropped in the other day to see Joe Shearer, the son—I had not seen him in thirty years. He said, "I would know your voice anywhere." During the talk I told him about the deal with his father, and said, "Surely you would not have that sin on your father's soul, owing me $8.33 all these years. Don't you think you ought to square it?" He said, "Yes, I'll pay it, but I'll be damned if I pay the interest on it for all these thirty years."

E. S. Brown was the leading merchant in Fall River. I believe he was another Wannamaker or Marshall Field or would have been in their class if fate had put him in their territory. He was on Main Street and his store was leased by R. A. McWhirr, so Brown leased an old theater to put his goods in while building a suitable place for his business. He went out to the extreme north while all the business was in the south and there he did business of a million a year. This was a great volume of business for a city like Fall River thirty-five or forty years ago. I wrote several notices of his window displays to help his advertising man, who was also a window-dresser. Each time they were printed the advertising man would put them on Brown's desk. Brown read them, "Pretty good, Jimmy, your pay will be two dollars a week more."

Then I wrote the life of E. S. Brown, epitomizing the story in about three or four thousand words, and had the good sense to send him the story before it was published. He just made one change in it. I said that he was the owner with the Claflin & Company, New York, and he wrote the word "sole" owner. After this story was printed he asked to see me and we became very firm friends. He wanted me to leave Fall River, go to Boston or New York, where he had friends in the big stores, and would get me into the advertising department.

He had a relative who was a congressman, and the congressman would aid me. But I was timid. I told him I was afraid. I was the only advertising man that Brown would talk to and our talk was usually on the floor of his fine store. Once, while we were chatting, a salesman tried to sell him some linen napkins. He said he was not interested, but the salesman said that they were wonderful value Irish linen napkins and the price was very low. Brown said that he was not interested. The salesman evidently knew him very well and he asked why he wasn't interested. Brown said, "The people of this town do not know what tablecloths are, let alone napkins." Brown bought for all his departments, but I chided him on this and said it was too much for him. He said that God was good to him, but the next day he got a paralytic stroke and never entered the store again.

The business fell into the hands of the bookkeeper, Dyer, Peckham the silk buyer, and MacFarland the carpet buyer. These men made quite an increase in the business, but I think MacFarland died, Peckham left and Dyer got a better job, so the business after that was not so good. For years this great, magnificent store has been empty. They can't even find tenants for it.

I have a kindly remembrance of a lovely woman who conducted a large specialty store. She was a Mrs. Nickerson. The beginning of her business was in a mill tenement and when I met her she was probably doing a $200,000 a year business. She was a very amiable, lovable, kindly woman who took an interest in everyone, at least she took a great interest in me. When she found that I had a great desire to see New York, she told me her brother-in-law was captain of a freight boat that plied between New Bedford and New York, and she would fix it up with the Captain to take me over and back. The captain was a delightful fellow and afterwards became admiral of the fleet of the New England Navigation Company. I shared his cabin with him and in the morning we had breakfast together. This was the first time I ever saw cantaloupe or small melon. There may have been people in Fall River who ate them, but I never saw them in any of the stores. We, in Fall River, lived on simple fare.

When the boat docked in New York I took a car for the Museum of Fine Arts. To see this and to see Niagara Falls had been the great dream of my life. I had with me my little handbag, as I planned on skipping one trip of the boat and then going home with the captain. In a little while we got to the Museum of Fine Arts as it was about to open. A big, rough policeman hailed me and said, "Boy, where are you going with that bag?" He explained it was forbidden to bring any articles into the museum. I suppose this must have been before the days of checking articles. I laid my valise at his feet and without a word started up the stairs of the museum; he called me back, pointed to the bag, and said, "How about this?" I said, "You won't let me bring it in; you're the policeman—you watch it." He laughed and looked me over and said, "Here, boy, we will put it behind the door; I don't think anyone will steal this."

I stayed about six hours in the museum. It was probably the most wonderful treat that has ever come to me. I looked for the masterpieces, Michael Angelo, Rubens, Van Dyke and the other great artists of which I had read. My two days in New York I spent in this wonderful museum, and I have often visited it since that time. I have seen many of the great museums of fine arts from here to San Francisco. I have always been fond of pictures and of nice things. I can hardly ever now pass a picture store without looking to see if there is anything that I have not seen before.

Once on my rounds in Boston I saw a picture of John L. Sullivan in the window of a deserted saloon, and in a religious store adjoining a picture of His Holiness, the Pope. The thought came to me that after all, men, like water, seek a level and they were appropriately placed. That of John L. in the deserted saloon and that of the Pope in an establishment catering to the finest things in life. The greatest picture that I ever saw was not a painting but a live picture. I have seen such a picture at least fifty times and never have I seen it without a lump coming into my throat. It is when the little boys and girls all in the innocent age, that is before they are seven, preceding the priest in the procession of the Blessed Sacrament. To see these hundreds of little boys as innocent as when they came from heaven and hundreds of little girls all dressed in white, with baskets of flowers, throwing them in the aisle in honor of the King of Kings. The saddest picture that I have seen, and I have seen sin and sickness and sorrow in many of its forms, is when the little tots from the Home for Destitute Catholic Children line up at the altar rail and when the people are asked to give these forlorn little creatures a home for a few weeks, a month or a longer period. The mute appeal in the faces of these little boys and girls is such as to bring tears to my eyes and a lump in my throat, and I bow my head to hide my emotions.

I have seen many wonderful things in this country of ours. I have lingered at the Grand Canyon, the greatest and most magnificent sight in this world, and I have seen the majesty and beauty of the Canadian Rockies, but never have I seen anything which impressed me as those two pictures of the little children that I have described.

CHAPTER VII

The earlier mills in Fall River all had entrance towers, but when the Stafford mill was erected it had no tower. Foster Stafford, the Treasurer, explained to a newspaper reporter who queried him on the subject that his mill had no tower because towers paid no dividends. Some years afterward Stafford erected in the Oak Grove Cemetery a monument; it was a replica of the Stafford Mills in miniature. There were the six stories, the numerous windows, the peaked roof and every detail of the mills to which he gave his life. Under this stone he was to rest until Gabriel summoned him forth. Stafford was proud of this monument and invited his fellow mill agents to come to see it. They looked it over and George Hill of the Devoll mills said to him rather dryly, "Foster, there is one thing missing in this monument." "A tower?" snapped Foster. "No," said Hill, "but when I think of the life you have led, I think you should have put fire escapes on it." Foster Stafford lies under this monument. I don't know where he went, but I know his mills went where Hill thought Stafford was going.

My cousin was the superintendent of these mills for nearly forty years. The one mill grew to three. I suppose the investment grew upwards of $2,000,000. When I was a boy in the mill, we would see the superintendent maybe two or three times a year, but my cousin was the first on the job every morning. He raced through the mills, up and down stairs of the three mills a half dozen times a day. In other words, he was on the job all of the time. He became the biggest stockholder in these mills. I know he held 760 shares. One day a segment of the flywheel of the engine flew off and went through the ceiling into the room overhead. The flywheel of the engine in a mill must be about 30 feet in diameter. It is put together in segments, maybe eight or ten, which are fastened on to the arms of the great wheel. This carries the main belt which drives the entire machinery. After the accident the insurance adjuster came to adjust damages and they said, "Mr. Sullivan, we'll give you a new segment of the wheel and repair the hole in the ceiling, and you might paint the whole engine room and send us the bill," but my cousin insisted on an entire new wheel. "Why?" the insurance man wanted to know. "Our men from Tech have just been here and tested the other segments and everything is all right, and we can't allow you any more than what we have allowed you; in fact, I think we have been very generous." Sullivan said, "This engine will never start while I am manager of this mill until I get a new wheel." The insurance company put it up to their lawyer, John W. Cummings, who was also my cousin's personal attorney. "What is the matter with you, Tim, that you don't accept the adjustment?" asked Cummings. "Well," Tim said, "last summer when we were building a new mill I used to sit out and watch the men at work. I saw a mason measure a stone for the capstone of the arch. He took a piece of granite and hit it with his hammer where he wanted it to break. He hit it twelve times and on the twelfth stroke the stone was broken. Now, Cummings, I know it wasn't the twelfth stroke nor the eleventh but each time he hit it, it injured the fabric of the stone that held it together. This being so, I know that the other segments of the wheel are not perfect. I don't know how much they have been injured, but at least to some extent. I insist on a new wheel." "You win," said Cummings.

In the course of time the new wheel came, and in unbolting the old one they found two of the segments had been cracked and if the engine had been started there would have been a disaster. I think this was the greatest selling illustration I ever heard. We talk to a man and he turns us down and we talk to him time and again, each time destroying the fabric of his resistance until we win his business. I also see in this story another illustration of how men can go wrong.

A temptation not resisted helps to destroy the fabric of character until some desperate thing is done. The mind is corrupted from the bad things introduced in our fiction. The youth and the maiden who read some of this so-called "sex stuff" that is now flooding not only our magazines but the stories in our newspapers are being harmed because the texture of their characters is being destroyed by repeated hammerings of those unclean authors.

I have been back to Fall River many times since I left there 32 years ago. I love Fall River. There my father and mother sleep side by side. Three of my brothers are resting in an adjoining grave. Below the hill my eldest boy is buried. I know he is with the angels.

When I left the Globe it was a great money-maker. In my solicitations in Boston and Providence and other cities I used to tell the space buyer it was the only paper in the country that declared a dividend every fifteen minutes. They had a beautiful building on Main Street, didn't owe a dollar, and their stock was valued at three hundred dollars a share. A humble curate of St. Mary's church, the Reverend Father

Cassidy, who afterward became Bishop of Fall River, brought the Globe to its knees. He gave a talk to his Holy Name Society about the evils of the saloon. He told of the sin and sorrow, misery and suffering, that these were doing to his people, and he asked them to vote for prohibition. We then had local option in Massachusetts. It was a really wonderful talk that this priest made and the News and Herald published it in full. The next week the good father gave a similar talk, going over the whole subject again, and once more asking the men of the Holy Name Society to help him abolish the saloon.

The Herald and the News published the entire text of his address, but in the Globe, the Catholic newspaper in Fall River, there was not a single notice of it. In his third address Father Cassidy said he was asked why the Globe didn't print his article, and he said the reason was simply the Globe was owned by liquor dealers and it represented liquor interests. The Globe, the following night, published an editorial of about two inches denouncing Father Cassidy. The next day its circulation dropped off more than one-half. Its advertising patronage began to decline and from that day the Globe never made a dollar; when Kelly took it over it was $240,000 in debt. I always believe that it is well to help those who are doing God's work. If you cannot help them, place no hindrance in their way, for in all conflicts God is helping those who are trying to do His work.

There was much drunkenness among the mill operatives in my time. Long hours of work, and insufficient food, led many into the saloons for a stimulant to restore their jangling nerves. They did not know that a glass of hot milk was the greatest nerve tonic. Even

AN IRISH BOY IN AMERICA

a cup of hot tea or coffee would have been better than alcoholic drinks to bring the nerves back to normal.

The favorite drink of the English was beer, which made them dull, stupid and sleepy. The Irish drank whiskey, which made them mad. The saloon-keeper's score had to be settled first on pay day. What was left went to the ill-kept wife and children.

There were mill employees who did not drink and their sons and daughters were educated and went into business or the professions.

The cotton mills in Fall River and there were no others, have experienced hard times. Few of the mills paid dividends in the last few years. Many of them are closed and gone into bankruptcy. The Granite mills, where I spent ten years as a boy, are bankrupt. Mill No. 1, which was the scene of the dreadful fire in '74, has been stripped of its machinery and it stands there idle and bare almost as it did after the great fire. No. 2 is silent. No. 3 is in the hands of another owner. The Stafford Mills are offered for $1.00 a share, but no one offers to buy. The three mills are closed. They will never resume. Thirteen years ago my cousin was offered $200 per share on this stock and he refused to sell because he claimed it was worth a great deal more.

Tim Sullivan, born in Portlaw and raised in Clonmel, was a remarkable man. His mother and mine were sisters. His mother was the eldest of twelve; my mother was the youngest girl and the eleventh child. I don't believe that Tim Sullivan ever broke one of the Ten Commandments in his life. He was a tall, handsome man and many a girl must have set her cap for him, but he could only see the mill. He was very religious, faithful in church attendance, gave freely to every call of the church and has given some wonderful gifts to the sisters in various convents.

I remember the engineer of the Stafford mills asking Tim Sullivan for a loan of two hundred dollars; he explained that he wanted to send his boy to college to become a priest. Tim refused him, said he never advanced money to anyone. The next day Tim sent for him and said, "Send your boy to college and send me all his bills from now until he is ordained." This was done and probably cost my cousin more than $10,000. I saw this young priest for the first time at the funeral of my cousin and afterwards had the good fortune to meet him; I believe the $10,000 was very well invested and paid Tim better dividends than any mill stock that he had.

The Laurel Lake mills, where I served my apprenticeship as a machinist, are gone. The New Bedford Standard published some years ago the names of the twenty-three corporations that were going and showed the average stock value of these to be thirty-five dollars a share; now about $7. What the future of this fine city will be, God only knows. Homer Loring, who rehabilitated the Boston and Maine Railroad, has taken a great interest in the city. After the disastrous fire he united five of the banks and purchased several of the mills for as much per cent of their original valuation. These manufacturers thought the mills would go on forever. They forgot that styles change with the times. When styles changed they didn't have machinery which would permit them to manufacture what the trade called for, nor did they have any money set aside to put in the required machinery. This stoppage of the mills has of course reduced valuation, with the result that taxes have been advanced to $42.50 per thousand, probably the highest rate in the country. This tax rate is not attractive to manufacturers who would like to go to Fall River where they can buy mills cheap. Maybe Lovering or a similar fine mind can find a solution, but it is beyond me. I do hope for the sake of those who remain that Fall River will again experience good times.

It looks as though the city is coming back. Men of financial and manufacturing genius assure me that this is so. There are now 236 industrial plants with a capital of $100,000,000. There are 22,000 workers, 15,000 being employed in the cotton textile plants. Many of the mills are working double shifts, so while there are not as many spindles, the production per spindle is greater. With a payroll of $60,000,000 it is far from being broke.

The city is now directed by a finance commission appointed by the governor. They have reduced all salaries, eliminated all waste and kept the expenses within the income, thus avoiding bankruptcy.

CHAPTER VIII

When I was on the Globe six years or so, a little item appeared in the newspapers that the New York, New Haven Railroad would electrify the trains between Fall River and Providence, and instead of running two or three trains a day, they would run more than twenty and the fare would be reduced from fifty cents to twenty cents. I told Kelly I would go to Providence and get enough business from the department stores to offset the loss of the business of E. S. Brown, the largest advertiser in town. Some months before Kelly had a run-in with Brown and we lost his business.

I went to Providence every Thursday for sixteen weeks and told the various advertising managers of the big stores about the great number of people who would come from Fall River to shop in Providence, because the big city always lured buyers from the smaller cities. Now with a round trip for forty cents and a reduction in the running time from forty-two to twenty-five minutes, a lot of buyers would come with money in their pockets. The first time I told my story to them they laughed and said there was nothing to it. Every week I called on the same men and told them the same story, and finally it dawned on them that I was right.

The first sale I made in Providence for the Globe was to Anthony Cowell and Company, a column a day for $650. These people sold high-grade furniture. Mr. Cowell said that after he made the contract with me quite a few people told him he should have purchased space in the News, as all the rich people in Fall River read it. Mr. Cowell asked these good people why the News did not come and tell him before he had made a contract with the Globe.

Then I sold the Outlet, the Boston store, O'Gorman's and others.

This electrical railroad, one of the finest in the country, is now a piece of junk, and Providence advertisers no longer advertise in the Fall River papers, but they do spend about $60,000 a year in the Pawtucket Times, because there is good transportation between the cities.

The owner of the O'Gorman store sent for me. He said he had $10,000 invested in the Providence News and he wanted me for advertising manager. Sharkey, his advertising manager, told him of my coming in every week for four months and he did everything but throw me out and the first thing he knew I was getting half pages and pages out of him.

I told him any solicitor could sell a good proposition if he saw the advertiser often enough and left him so that he could go back in a week and make another plea. Men fail because they do not keep at the job. O'Gorman said that sounded good to him and to see G. W. Brown, the owner of the News, and make a contract with him on my own terms.

I left Fall River in May, 1903, and in December, Mary and the two babies came over the bridge that spans the beautiful Taunton River to join me in Providence. We had a beautiful home there and we thought we would spend many a pleasant year in that fine city. But fate willed it otherwise and in a few years we moved on to Pittsburgh, Cleveland, Chicago, Boston, New York and then back to Boston where we have taken root deep down in the ground. We love it so well that here we stay unless God wills otherwise.

I have not met Kelly to talk with since I resigned from the Globe, but see how the pendulum swings. Three or four months after my leaving Fall River, he was discharged. I brought the business into the paper and when I resigned business stopped coming in. An outstanding friend told Kelly if he could get a little money he could buy a place in the Smith Thompson Agency, and this was brought about. In a little while they got the Boston Post on a small salary, now grown to a handsome amount and from time to time added papers to the agency list.

In a short time he became sole owner and built up a list of powerful daily newspapers because of his popularity and knowledge of advertising and newspaper management. In the 25 years he amassed a substantial fortune.

When I was with Julius Mathews I was negotiating with the Hartford Times. Chamberlain came up to see Marchant of the Post, a very dear friend of mine, and asked which agency he should take, Kelly or Julius Mathews. Marchant advised Kelly and said, "I did this, Dave, for Kelly was poor and your boss was rich." Well, about six years ago Kelly bought the Herald and News, combined the two, and got a new building. The investment was $750,000 and then he went over and bought the Globe and united the three of them at the cost of a million dollars, so the youth that was considered no good now owns every daily newspaper that is published in Fall River.

Kelly has probably changed from the time I knew him. Maturity surely developed wisdom and with wisdom comes charity and kindliness. The first day he was on the Herald-News, he said to the manager, "These employees are all underpaid—advance their pay, everyone on the paper, ten per cent." So this confirms in my mind the belief that when he got out in the world, away from parsimonius influence, the good in him rose to the surface.

I understand that his paper in Fall River makes a net profit of about $100,000 a year. While he keeps a watchful eye on it, most of his time is given to the direction of his agency in New York, Chicago, Philadelphia, Detroit, Atlanta and Boston.

Brown gave me a year's contract at fifty dollars per week and twenty-five per cent of the increase. I only had his contract a week or so when I found I was doing business with a man who was queer. The News, according to the affidavit, had 9600 daily circulation and the Bulletin had 54,000. I figured I could get at least ten dollars a reader. Nowadays circulation is worth from twenty dollars to twenty-five dollars a reader. The wise publisher who realizes this is always out after circulation, not for what the reader pays for it, but for the advertising value each reader has. When the Saturday Evening Post had 2,000,000 circulation its advertising was $24,000,000, or twelve dollars a reader. The New York Times has an advertising value of $44 per reader.

My friend Holfelder urged me not to make a contract with Brown. He said other good men had worked on the News and failed. Contracts had been broken and they had been unable to collect because he had a mortgage on the plant for four times its value. If they did get judgment against him, there was no money.

I told Holfelder the Governor would never break this contract. The first week I was there I asked the Governor to show me the 9600 copies every day that he had sworn to. "How much have I got?" he asked. "Less than half," I answered. "Now listen carefully to what I say, Governor. You have had good men here and they have been crushed between you and the advertiser. You lied to me about your circulation. I am going to stay here a year and don't you ever try any funny business on me, or you will be sorry, very sorry."

One morning the second or third week I was there, I came into the office at nine o'clock, as I did every morning. The Governor asked me if I couldn't get in earlier. I reminded him that when I made the contract I explained to him that Mary was expecting a visit from the stork and that I would not move to Providence until the baby came. I would leave my house in Fall River at seven and reach the office at nine. He had agreed to this, yes he admitted he agreed to it, but thought I ought to get there earlier. I asked him what time he expected me to come and he said that he got there every morning at six o'clock, which was true. I smiled and said, "Governor, do you expect me here at six?" He said he would like to have me there at seven. I said, "You made a mistake, Governor, when you hired me as an advertising manager—what you wanted was a janitor."

Two or three times during the year he invited me to resign and I graciously declined. We worked hard, tried to get what business we could, but I saw no chance for the News unless we made a paper equal or almost equal to the powerful Bulletin.

The Outlet was a great store in Providence. It was owned by the Samuels Brothers. They got fond of me and we worked out a plan for the Governor's approval. The common stock of the News was to be shared by O'Gorman and the Outlet. The bonds, about $150,000, were to be held by the Governor. Samuels and O'Gorman agreed to see that the interest was paid on the bonds and each of them would contribute $20,-

000 in display advertising. I was to be the sole manager of all departments. The Governor agreed and instead of losing $25,000 a year in the News he was to be practically granted $150,000 for a plant worth probably $25,000 or $30,000. This was a day or two before the expiration of my contract. That night going home I was his best friend. In the morning he denounced me. He would have nothing to do with the plan. I was trying to rob him of his paper. He would make a settlement with me. He said, "Your pay was to be fifty dollars a week, that is $2600 a year. I have paid you $2250. Here is my check for $350. Isn't that right? There is no commission due you because there has been no increase in business." But there had been an increase in business. The advertising of the Brown Mill Supply House Company and the real estate development on the Narragansett River, which the year before had been put on the books as cash, in my year were put on as a gratuity to the Governor, so the books would not show any increase in business. "Isn't this right?" said the Governor, and he handed me a check for $350. I said, "This is Leap Year and write me out a check for one more day." He did it with a smile, he was so glad to get rid of me.

Ten years later I met him at the Waldorf-Astoria. He walked up to me with the lovelight in his eye. He grasped my hand and said, "There, every man who worked for me became a great man."

He sold the News some few years later and the new owners told me when they took it over that it had a circulation of eighty-four copies. I always felt sorry for the Governor, for he wanted to be vice president of the United States and he felt that he had to have a newspaper. He was by no means a bad man, but he surely was away off as a newspaper publisher.

The Outlet boys had come over to Providence some years before and were considered fly-by-nights. Merchants who could come in for a month or so took the cream and skipped back to New York. The merchants in Providence got together and prevailed on the newspapers not to accept the advertising of these people. The Bulletin and the Journal would not accept a line. The Telegram refused in the beginning but afterwards accepted it. The Samuels brothers were furious. They hired twenty sandwich men to parade up and down in front of the Bulletin office with signs that read—"The Bulletin and the Journal will not accept our advertisements—ask them why!" They hired poster boards which carried this message and they carried it to such an extent that when one of the Samuels boys advertised for a maid, the Journal and the Bulletin would not even carry that.

This incensed the Samuels, and one day the Journal and Bulletin carried an advertisement of the New York Sunday American in half page space. The advertisement read: "Every man and woman in Providence should read page 14 of the Sunday American; there is something of vital interest to you." Page 14 contained a terrific attack on the Journal and the Bulletin from the Samuels boys. They surely did lambaste the two papers and from that day the Samuels prospered. From the little store they built a great department store that now does a business of probably $8,000,000. Some years ago they made an offer to the Bulletin for advertising, $100,000 a year. The Bulletin accepted it on the grounds that when they refused the business the manufacturers of the Outlet Company were a fly-by-night, but now they could accept it since they knew otherwise.

As the Bulletin had 50,000 readers this $100,000 was $2 a year a reader. While it is only two-thirds of a cent a day a family, I never knew a department store to pay as much. The big stores in Boston pay about 30 cents a family. That is a daily of say 300,000 circulation will get about 300,000 lines at about 30 cents a line. Newspaper advertising is cheap, very cheap and very good.

Any of the great dailies in Boston, the Post, Globe, Herald and American will give any retail advertiser a page a day, seven days a week for one and a half cents a family. If a merchant can't make this profitable there is something wrong with his copy or his store, probably the latter.

CHAPTER IX

I was out of work, but I never even thought of Fall River. When I left, C. S. Greene said there would always be a job on the Globe for me, and if I ever needed money to write to him and I could have it. I never even let the good man know that I was out of a position.

Charles Taylor of the Boston Globe put an advertisement in the Publishers' Confidential Bulletin for me. Charles and W. O., his brother, are always doing nice things for somebody and never saying anything about them. They have a great newspaper and use their men well. They hold their check books at the service of their employees in sickness or death. In answer to the advertisement which Mr. Taylor so kindly inserted for me I got a letter from the Pittsburgh Times, Milwaukee Sentinel, Minneapolis Journal, a paper in Duluth and one in Texas, one in Seattle and one from Haskell of the Boston Herald.

Swift of the Minneapolis Journal wanted me to see him in Chicago. I wired back I'd be in Chicago in two days. Charles Taylor gave me transportation as far as Albany and my friend Cox of the Manchester Union got transportation from Buffalo to Chicago and return. We newspaper advertising men were fond of one another and did little favors for one another when possible. I went to Chicago in the day coach all the way through. I didn't have any money for a Pullman, so sat up all night and played cards. In the morning I found that my clothes were not presentable and sent them out to be pressed.

AN IRISH BOY IN AMERICA 93

As I sat by my bedside in the hotel the following morning, I was informed that Mr. Swift of the Minneapolis Journal was downstairs and desired to see me. I sent down word that I was in conference and would join him in half an hour. I could not very well receive anyone as my clothes had not been returned by the tailor. In half an hour I met him and we talked together for an hour; he finally agreed to hire me on condition. He thought I was the man for the job and he would give me $60.00 per week as advertising manager of the Minneapolis Journal, provided I got the O. K. of his New York Special Agency man, M. Lee Starke. I said that he would approve because Starke had tried to hire me a year before. I explained to Swift that my transportation called for Boston, so I would have to ask him to give me transportation to New York so I could see Starke. He gave me a note to the passenger agent of the line which went to New York, and I presented the note to him. He said, "What position do you occupy on the Minneapolis Journal?" I said, "Advertising Manager."

I saw his lips move, and we who worked in the cotton mills all knew the lip language, and what he said was "You're a liar." He knew Sawyer was the advertising manager, had known him for twenty years, and hadn't heard of any change. I met Starke in New York, told him the story, and he said, "Sure, you're the man for the place; go home to Providence and I will write Swift." In a few days I got a wire from Starke saying, "Everything is lovely." He told me that he had written Swift a very fine letter of approval and Swift had agreed that I could be advertising manager but he had a contract with Sawyer which didn't expire until September first, whereas this was in the early part of June. Swift suggested that I work in Starke's office in the meantime, Swift paying $30.00 and Starke paying the other $30.00 until the first of September, when I was to take charge of the advertising. I told Starke this was agreeable to me. Starke said, "Fine, but I have a confession to make to you—I'm broke. I can't pay the $30.00 per week. I will pay your expenses if you can live on the $30.00 that Swift sends." I accepted the $30.00 a week and with that I had to keep myself in New York and my home in Providence.

I found a room in Brooklyn at three dollars a week and I allowed myself ten cents for carfare, ten cents for lunch, five cents for a couple of stogies. Had a lot of calls in New York, Pittsburgh, Philadelphia and Boston, for not only the Minneapolis Journal but for all the Starke papers. He had six, all fine papers—Washington Star, Montreal Star, Indianapolis News, Baltimore Sun and Newark News. Each paid him $100 a week, and I couldn't understand why he was broke, but it seems he was tied up in some manufacturing enterprise up the Hudson and this took all his money. Starke and I became great friends. He said I had great ability and was a great advertising man.

At the end of two months he came to me, his face all white. "That blankety-blank Swift has thrown you and me over and hired McKinley Barber as advertising manager of the Minneapolis Journal. You write him to continue your pay until September first as per agreement." Looking back, the letter I wrote must have scorched the soul of Swift. I never met him again but I have forgiven him.

I then wrote Sief of the Pittsburgh Times and he came on to see me. He said that the Times was owned by the Magee estate and when Chris Magee was alive the Times was a very prosperous newspaper and easily the leading one in Pittsburgh. Magee was a political

AN IRISH BOY IN AMERICA 95

boss much like Richard Croker in New York. George Oliver of Pittsburgh wanted to become United States Senator and he established the Chronicle, Telegraph and the Gazette, and these papers took away a lot of the Times business. For some reason that Mr. Sief would not understand, twenty-eight of the big advertisers were out of the Times and he wanted to know what I thought of the situation. I asked him about the circulation and he said he had 68,000. Asked him what the Gazette Telegram had and he didn't know nor did he know what the Dispatch or Post had, the other morning papers in Pittsburgh. He felt sure that he had the most circulation, but he did know the other papers were carrying the business and the Times was not. I told him that it looked to me as though his circulation was in doubt with the merchants and as they bought values, they probably felt that when Magee died the paper lost circulation. Sief said that could not be so as he published his sworn net paid circulation at the top of his editorial columns every day. I asked him to send to my home in Providence a copy of all the morning papers, a rate card, and the "literature" of the Times and other papers being sent to the advertisers.

In a few days the papers, rate cards, etc., arrived, and I looked over the Times and found it a very excellent newspaper compared to the Post, but the Gazette and Telegraph were really very well done. The Dispatch had every earmark of being made up by bright men who were conducting its destinies. Looking over the matter sent out by the Times to the advertiser, the first piece that came to my hand was a letter from the advertising manager of the Joseph Horn Company, the greatest department store in Pittsburgh, to Mr. Sief, the publisher of the Times. When I read it I laughed and said to Mary, "I have found what the trouble with the Times is." This letter from the advertising manager, Mr. Hammond, stated that he had an argument with the advertising solicitor of another paper. Hammond maintained the Times had a circulation exceeding 65,000 but the advertising solicitor maintained it only had 18,000. The letter went on to say that Hammond slipped in one night and watched the press run off the Times and saw that it was printing over 68,000 copies. I wrote to Sief that the trouble was in his case that the viewpoint of the advertising solicitor was similar to that held by the space buyers in Pittsburgh rather than what Hammond had found to be true. I explained to him that the merchants bought on the reputation of the paper rather than on its character, and while these two usually went hand in hand, in the case of the Times they did not.

This letter impressed Sief so much that he invited me to come as advertising and business manager at a salary of $60.00 per week. I wrote him for a contract and he wrote back a very nice letter that that was unnecessary. The editor had been there thirty years, Jones twenty and Chambers eighteen, etc., so a contract would not be necessary. I accepted the position and one Sunday morning I arrived in Pittsburgh with my wife, my two children, my two sisters-in-law, a dog and a five-dollar bill.

Shortly after we were married, Mary, who was the eldest child of her family, took her three sisters and her brother under her wing, and two of these girls have been with us almost all the time for the forty years of our married life. They have amply paid me for the care we gave them by love and affection during all these years.

Our first thought that Sunday morning was to get

to Mass. Mary and I went to the first Mass, then we asked the good God to care for us and to guide our actions in this great and strange city of Pittsburgh. The two girls went to the following Mass and they and my good wife and I went looking for a boarding house. Sixty dollars at a hotel would hardly pay for the board of the six of us. We boarded for a while then we took a furnished apartment, where we were very happy. I might say that we have enjoyed more happiness than anyone that I know. We never had a great deal of money, but more joy, more of the good things of life have come to us than to any couple that I know. This is Mary's thought as well as mine; she doesn't know any woman who has had one-half the good time she has had in our forty years of marriage, and there has never been a single word of discord between us, in fact between myself and any member of the household.

The first few weeks on the Times I made a survey of the situation. I talked to various clerks, buyers in the stores, who didn't know I was connected with the Times, and they all told me the Times was a third rater. We had two or three advertising solicitors who went out daily and came back with nothing. They were fairly good men but they seemed to me to be beaten. I asked one of them one day about some account and he said the merchants said what was the use of giving advertising to the Times, it was going out of business pretty soon, and George Oliver was going to own it. I asked Sief about this and he said some time before George Oliver had come in to see him and told him he wanted to purchase the Times. Sief told him the paper was not for sale, but Oliver said, "A man will sell anything but his wife or daughter, so put a price on it." This Sief did and asked for $1,700,000, which was a pretty stiff price for a paper in Pittsburgh thirty-two years ago. Oliver told Sief he would hear from him later. Sief said he did, but in an indirect way—the hammering started against the Times. He could see there was an organized attack to put the Times out of business, but he was helpless. Word had come back to Sief from Oliver that when Oliver wanted the Times he would buy it at his own price.

I told Sief I was pretty good at throwing bricks myself, and for every brick that was thrown at the Times I would see that there were two bricks thrown through the panes of glass in his windows. We had a circulation manager named Herreck, a very able and capable man. I told him that I wanted the circulation in detail of the Gazette, the Post, the Dispatch and the Times. He didn't know just how to get them. I said, "Listen, Herreck, every paper published must go somewhere; it must be sold by news dealers or by newsboys. It must be sold in the city or country or on the streets or in the hotels. You give me a memo showing the distribution of the Times in every source and in parallel columns give me the same story about the other paper."

About this time I received a letter from my brother Jim, who was a printer in Fall River. He had been the mill man for thirty years, a very skilled man of great ability, and was the first man in New England to run compound engines. He had purchased a printing plant and in addition to his job work was running the Catholic Advocate, a wonderfully fine weekly newspaper. Jim wrote that Fall River was in the dumps owing to a long strike and asked if I could help him to get a job. When Jim was master mechanic of the Laurel Lake Mill I was his apprentice. He was then getting $3.50 a day and I $1.00; he had paid for a course of instructions for me in night business college and had done many a kindly turn for me. I wired him I was sending him transportation for Pittsburgh and there was a job here for him at $30.00 a week as my assistant. When he arrived he got right on the job, and he wanted to know from the advertiser who, when, why, where and what. He got business too. He also found that to get legal business in the State of Pennsylvania the law required the filing of a sworn net paid circulation in some department of State in Allegheny City.

Jim went over and copied the statements. The sworn net paid for the Dispatch was 45,000, the Post somewhere in the neighborhood of 40,000, the Gazette 62,000. Our net paid was 68,000 so I felt I had the ammunition for a real fight. I got the figures from our circulation man showing every avenue of distribution, and this showed that the Times led them all except in street sales. It is an odd thing, but the newspaper finds its best circulation in street sales, and as many of the advertisers saw what was true of the street sales they thought this must be necessarily true of the home circulation. Hence the Times, a great newspaper, lost the business which went to the other papers.

I compiled about twelve typewritten pages much like my friend Clark did when he compiled his lessons on hypnotism. The first pages dealt with the home delivered circulation and the street sales, country distribution, news dealers, etc. Then a letter from an advertising bureau which is similar to our A. A. A. stating that the Times had been examined by them, and there followed an analysis of circulation showing the sworn net paid of a trifle over 68,000. Next page contained foreign net paid as filed in Allegheny of the Post, Gazette and Dispatch. When this was finished and ready to go out, the superintendent of schools came in and I got him to write me a letter about the character of the Times, which was to finish up the booklet. It was a really wonderful letter. This was sent to everyone in a store in Pittsburgh. Every advertising manager, every buyer in a store, and the twenty advertising agents in Pittsburgh who wrote local accounts and sent this booklet out through the country. The next morning Sief told me he had a telephone call from Mr. Barr, the publisher of the Pittsburgh Post. He said that the figures given the Post were wrong and he would have Lawlor arrested for such a libelous piece of work. I told Sief to telephone Barr and tell him that we didn't wish to do him any injury, but if he would send over a statement of circulation we would print it.

The next visitor was the superintendent of schools, who said that every newspaper publisher in town had called up and abused him, and he requested that I not print his letter again. Barr sent over his figures and the only thing to increase his circulation a few thousands was to swell the street sales, so in the booklet issued a few days later, after each figure of the Post was a star, and at the foot of the page, "Official figures furnished by the Pittsburgh Post." This last offense was the worst, for it nearly drove the Post out of business.

The day the first figures were published, Morris Baer, manager of Kaufman's Department Store, sent for me. He opened the book and said, "Are these figures right?" I said, "To the best of my knowledge and belief." He was very excited and said, "Listen, boy, if these figures are correct I will give George Oliver and the Chronicle Telegram a slap on the wrist that he will remember for many days." He was running a page every day in the Chronicle Telegram, one-half page in the Gazette and a couple of pages in the Sunday Gazette. He was probably their greatest advertiser. He sent for me again in a couple of hours and said, "I guess you are wrong in your statements; I phoned the Pittsburgh Gazette and they stated that you have credited them with only 400 circulation in East Liberty when they have 750. If you are that much out of the way in one point, they say the whole picture was cockeyed." I explained to Baer that it was quite possible that there was an error there, as we had some difficulty in getting those figures. Our circulation man said his men had got the conductor drunk, but in counting the papers on the run the motorman had interfered and there had been a fight. I said, "Baer, if you want to know the truth, just drop into the business office of the Gazette and ask for the galley proofs on circulation. Every bundle that goes out has a sticker giving the dealer's name and the number of papers that go to him. Total up those galley proofs and you will find that I am right on circulation." This was done while I was there, and the galley proofs showed that I was within ten of the circulation of the Gazette.

Baer withdrew all his advertising from the Gazette and Telegram and the Sunday paper. Some time a year or so afterward the boys on the other paper told me that I sure had raised merry hell in Pittsburgh. The merchants refused to pay the advertising debts, claiming they had been sold on 100,000 circulation and they had bought it on that basis and would pay pro rata or not at all. This I didn't know at the time, but I knew the enemy was being injured.

Every day I had sent out an illustrated postcard to every store owner or advertising manager, and every power in the advertising agencies, telling how the Times guaranteed more circulation in the city of Pittsburgh and out of Pittsburgh than any other morning newspaper. Every day I had a different illustration made by the artist in some one of the agencies, never the same agency twice, so that in twenty-eight days I had seen the twenty-eight agencies, made friends and left them the price of the illustration. Then followed a list showing quality circulation. The names and addresses of one hundred subscribers of the Times who were rated in Dun and Bradstreet's as millionaires.

This shows what a wonderful town Pittsburgh was for making money. It was dirty—so dirty that when you went to the barber shop to have a shave, before the barber could shave you he would get a pail of water and big sponge and begin to rub you over to see your face. Even the books in the steel safe were dirty. You could never keep the dirt of Pittsburgh out, but there were a lot of good men and women in Pittsburgh. The merchants used me royally when they saw the fight that was going on. Of the twenty-eight bigger accounts out, fourteen had come back, twelve of them were mightily interested and said they would be back in a little while.

One advertising agent, who had been quite hostile, told me that he had a Jewish client who said to him, "I guess we will have to use the Times—I wish you would make arrangements for it." The advertising man asked him why, as there had been no change. "Well," the old merchant said, "I guess we should go into the Times; I hear it discussed at the Duchesne Club," so he said the business would follow in the course of a week or two. Then Sief got what the boys call "cocky." He wanted to raise the rates on those who had been out. I told him this was wrong, that we must first get

AN IRISH BOY IN AMERICA 103

the volume, that rates could always be raised on the volume of business. Everything was lovely and the fight seemed to be about over when I found a note on my desk one day from Mr. Sief asking for my resignation on the ground that I didn't get along with the editorial force. I had been there five months and never had but a pleasant greeting from the editor. There had been no conflict, no question. I went in to see Sief and said, "How about this?" He said, "Don't ask any questions. Saturday night I will give you two weeks' pay and I am sorry." I showed the note to my brother. He had more fire in his makeup than I have. He said just four words and they were very expressive, but they would not look well in print.

I never knew why Sief betrayed me. When a man does an injury to another man it is usually due to bad kidneys or a bad conscience. Oliver sent me word I could have a job on his paper, but I asked that he put me in the real estate bureau in Pittsburgh. Before this could be done, I made an engagement with the Ohio Baking Company.

Some little while afterward, George Oliver came over to see Sief and said, "There is the cashier's check for $1,700,000." Sief said, "Here is your paper," took his coat and went out. The next day the Times and the Gazette were consolidated. It is my belief that the deal was put through while I was on the Times but my commissions on the sale was a discharge with two weeks' pay. The advertising manager of Kaufman's store sent for me and said, "I was told you are through with the Times." I said, "Yes." He said, "I was telling an official of the Ward Macky Company about you last night and he wants to see you. I told him about the man from Boston that made Pittsburgh sit up and take notice, so I think you can get what you want from these people."

CHAPTER X

I had known Caufrain for some little time. One day going through my desk I found some proofs of advertisements in the Times. Very logical and very well done they were. I asked who wrote this brilliant copy and they said an old fool that worked here by the name of Caufrain. I located him with a quack doctor. When I told him I would like to meet him on account of the brilliance of his work, that I felt that he was a master workman and was surprised to find such wonderful copy, he explained that he had been advertising manager of a big concern in Buffalo for many years and that conditions made him go to work for Campbell's, a fourth rate department store. The boys in the advertising department of the newspaper gave him a banquet when he had been there about a month and when it came his turn to speak he spoke about the wonderful papers in Pittsburgh and he wondered why, where there were so many fine papers, they allowed a fourth or fifth rater like the Times to exist. It seemed to him that they ought to put it out of business. The Times man explained his mistake and he had a talk with Sief. Caufrain thought he should be able to do something for the Times so he wrote these advertisements. Sief kept him three weeks and then discharged him. He proposed a plan to Morris Baer for his advertising and after looking up his record Caufrain was engaged to come to work the following Monday morning as advertising manager of Kaufman's. "I will see that the Times gets its share of the business," said Caufrain, in spite of his abrupt dismissal.

I saw the copy that Caufrain proposed for the Kaufman's stores. I never saw its equal. I knew Powers and Manley Gillam, who wrote the Wannamaker copy which made them famous throughout the country, but they were not the equals of Caufrain. He was a marvelous advertising man, not only as a copy writer but as a thinker. He said that it was his plan that there should be two advertising managers of the store—one to write for the morning newspapers and one for the evening newspapers, as the clientele of each paper was different.

While I was on the Times some advertising manager somewhere on an evening paper sent out a booklet far and wide proving to his satisfaction that the evening paper gave better results than the morning newspaper. In this booklet were letters from merchants in various cities telling how they preferred evening papers, and there were four or five letters from merchants in Fall River telling why they preferred evening papers instead of morning papers. I wrote to this author and said, "You poor man, I know Fall River and there has not been a morning paper there in twenty years. The only morning paper they ever had in the whole existence of the city only lasted five months." He never answered me but I wrote a defense of the morning paper that we sent all over the country. It does not make much difference whether a paper is published morning or evening. If it is a great paper it will produce for advertisers. In New York the Times is a morning paper and in Philadelphia the Bulletin is published in the evening. In Chicago, the Tribune is a great morning newspaper and the News is a fine newspaper published in the evening. In Providence the evening Bulletin towers over the morning Journal owned by the same people. In Boston the morning Post is very powerful and the same can be said of the Globe, which is both morning and evening and sold for the one price. There is a tendency for high grade copy to go into the morning papers, and sales and basement advertising to go into the evening papers. Of it a notable exception is the Boston Evening Transcript, which carries a full line of high grade advertising.

I went to see the bakery people. First question was, "Can you write?" I said, "Yes." "Write me a booklet of this bakery and see me tomorrow," he added, and dismissed me with a wave of his hand. It was some job to write the booklet of a business that you didn't know. I walked through the bakery, a great big affair, baking thirty or forty different kinds of bread and fifty or sixty kinds of crackers.

There were machines I had never seen before in my life and I didn't know what it was all about nor just where to begin. I learned that a party was to be shown through that night, so Mary and I went with the party. We began where the flour came in from the cars. We were told about the machines where the flour was sifted through a fine silk cloth and then went to the mixer, where yeast, salt, shortening, milk and water were added. It was pointed out to us that this machine had six arms and that it turned 1720 times. This would have heated the dough and the yeast would have begun to work before the mixing was complete, but a current of cold air was introduced into the mixer from the refrigerator. Then the dough was laid out in a room to rise and this room had a temperature winter and summer of eighty-four degrees. The yeast would be in the best condition to work at that temperature.

Then we followed the dough to the bench where it was moulded into loaves (the work of skillful men). We were told that no machine could replace the human hand for this work, although now every loaf is moulded by machine. We were shown the proof rooms and then the ovens heated by natural gas, and then we saw the bread pulled out and placed in cooling racks. Then there was an army of workmen in a big bakery hut; today there is hardly a corporal's guard, as about everything is done by machinery.

When the guide had finished I saw that the sequence was the same as I had seen when a boy in Daly's Bake Shop, where less than one hundred loaves a day were baked. In the morning I captured this man who took us through the night before and asked him to explain some things that were not clear in my mind, especially about the mixing machines. He brought me some printed matter. I wrote the story that morning, and the company liked it.

This booklet was afterward given wide circulation. In the story it was told that the heat of the oven was four hundred degrees, since a heat was necessary to kill the yeast germs. Twenty years afterward I was listening to an address by the President of Dartmouth College. He told his great audience that once he had read a very interesting booklet on a loaf of bread and it required an oven heat of four hundred degrees to kill the yeast germ, but now he finds Fleishmann using pages imploring people to take within themselves three or four yeast cakes a day, else they could never be healthy, wealthy or wise.

I was engaged to put on an advertising campaign in Cleveland. The plan was to put in one gold thimble and two silver ones, and having them baked in the dough and no one would know where the bread would go. The thought was to pay a reward of five dollars for the return of each silver thimble and ten dollars for the gold, the finders to keep the thimbles.

I was told to report in Cleveland and they would see me in a couple of weeks. My pay was to be thirty dollars a week. Quite a drop from sixty dollars, but half a loaf was better than no bread.

So I bade Pittsburgh goodby very reluctantly. Jim went back to Fall River and I started for Cleveland to find a home for Mary and the babies. Naturally I went to a boarding house instead of a hotel on account of the expenses. Half a dozen times I have had to live in boarding houses until I found a home for my people. Good people ran these houses and all were kind to me. Usually I had a room and kept my weight down by eating very lightly which was necessary anyway, owing to the lightness of my purse. It was no hardship, but the absence of my dear ones was felt very keenly.

In every city there is one man that we of the faith can turn to for advice and that is the parish priest. "So you want a furnished house for your family," and he smiled at me as he gave me a quick glance. "You can't pay much on a salary of thirty dollars a week. I would say that thirty dollars a month would be about right; one week's salary for a month's rent," he went on. "Every man should live in a house befitting his station in life. There is a family on Oakdale Street going away for six months and I believe you could have their house for about the sum you have in mind."

My family followed me shortly afterward, and during our stay in Cleveland we enjoyed the nice little house on Oakdale Street.

The advertising plan was there were to be three teaser advertisements of about 100 lines each. These three advertisements informed the people about the loss of the thimbles and the reward that was being offered for their recovery by the Second National Bank of Cleveland. Each of the advertisements contained an illustration of Mose Cleveland, that is the figure of an old man in knickerbockers, which was used much at that time to symbolize the City of Cleveland, as Uncle Sam is used to individualize the members of this great country. This was to be followed by one-half page advertisement showing that the thimbles were in loaves of Ward's bread.

My advice was to use every paper in Cleveland—the Plain Dealer, the News, the Leader and the German Anziger. These advertisements were set in the office of the Cleveland Plain Dealer and there I met a man whom I believe is one of the finest men in the United States, not only a fine man but a great newspaper man, Frank S. Baker, then advertising manager for his father but now owner of two of the great papers in Tacoma, Washington. We have been intimate friends for more than twenty-five years and I believe him to be the "salt of the earth."

The three teaser advertisements attracted a great deal of attention. It turned out the second National Bank knew nothing about the plan. The morning that the first advertisement broke in the Plain Dealer and the Leader, which were the two morning papers, I got a call from Mr. Baker. "Mr. Lawlor, the president of the Second National Bank is in my office and he sure is raising Cain." "Why? What about?" I asked. "Well, he said he didn't know anything about this gold and silver thimble racket and he is not offering any reward for their return." "I don't see what interest he has in the matter, because it is the First National Bank that is offering the rewards," I answered. Baker

AN IRISH BOY IN AMERICA 111

said, "I handled all the copy and I had a great interest in it; I know that you advertised the Second National Bank." "True," I replied, "we didn't want anyone to know the details of this plan, so we used the name of the Second National Bank as fiction, and last night while he was at dinner I changed this in the proof to the First National Bank, got proof from the office and all the other newspapers have the corrected copy."

I went down to the Plain Dealer's office. Mr. Baker was full of apologies. He explained that the girl proofreader was out to dinner when I made the changes and when the new copy came to her desk she knew it was an error, that the First National Bank name was wrong and she changed it back to the Second National Bank. Mr. Baker looked at the half page sorrowfully and said, "Too bad I lose that half page." "I don't see why you are going to lose it," I answered as I put my arm around his shoulder. "You mean you will O. K. this with the error about the bank?" "Sure, my boy, you have been kind to me, took good care of the copy, and you will get your money for the half page." Baker held out his hand, "Put it there, you are the first honest advertising man I have met."

Ward lost nothing by this act of decency. Men usually return kindness for kindness. Every advertisement of the Ohio Bakery Company (this was before it became a part of the present company) received full position in the Plain Dealer at run of paper rates.

I told the management that I found that of the 1100 dealers in Cleveland, we were only supplying 400 of them. "What of it, 400 is a good selling distribution," he answered. "Those 700 dealers have not got your bread so can't sell it. If they have it there is a chance of your selling it. Let me write to each of your dealers in your name and tell them about the proposed campaign. The day the first loaves are put on the market, let me send three loaves of bread to each of the 700 dealers and have them try it on their own tables," I answered. So when the campaign started we sent a series of five letters three days apart, telling the dealers about what was being done, the wonderful excellence of the bread, and that there would be many calls for the famous Tip-Top bread.

We ran about thirty pieces of copy in the newspapers three times a week for ten weeks and the sales of the bread jumped from ten thousand to forty thousand loaves a day. Out of the 1100 dealers, all handled the bread but two. The second week of the campaign the management told me there was much substitution, the dealers handing out the bread of other bakers when Tip-Top was called for, and he asked me to write the dealers a special letter. About that time Roosevelt was calling for a square deal and this letter to the dealers put this matter of substitution up to their honor. The day after this letter went out substitution ceased. Every man felt he had to look after his own honor and it was not honorable to substitute. At the end of six months the Ohio Baking Company was absorbed by the Ward Corby Company. This was the amalgamation of Ward Mackey and Ohio Baking and Corby Brothers of Washington. Corby Brothers were the inventors of the Corby Mixers, an important factor in the success of the Ward's. Ohio Baking Company manufactured crackers. I think there were about twenty or twenty-five salesmen selling within a radius of four or five hundred miles. Rothlesberger, the manager of the bakery, was to write to his salesmen and on my arrival turned these letters over to me to write. I think I wrote one a week for about thirty weeks. Rothlesberger thought they were wonderful and the salesmen were delighted with them because in each letter, in addition to the analysis of the goods and their comparison with similar goods, there were sales talks which they could use to the dealers they approached, but also in each letter was encouragement. There was no scolding, no fault-finding, but a spirit of appreciation and helpfulness.

The Chicago Tribune magazine section editor negotiated for a reprint of those but for some reason they never were published. In Cleveland I met Mr. R. B. Ward, the president. Robert B. Ward was not only a great business man but a very spiritual man.

He was the father of ten children, and they tell me he never entered his house without embracing his wife, for he was the lover as well as the husband. He told me that the new company were opening a bakery in Chicago and I was to go as advertising manager of the Ward Corby Company and open this bakery. They would increase my pay to forty dollars per week and pay my expenses.

I liked Cleveland; it was a beautiful city. Our advertising campaign was placed through the W. S. Hill Agency of Pittsburgh and Hill came on for a conference. Hill suggested that we use the popular newspapers in Chicago. I suggested that we use them all and both Ward and Hill opposed it. The executive said, "Dave, what is the matter with you; a loaf of bread baked in a bakery is bought by the poor men, not by the well-to-do, so why should we use the Tribune and the Record Herald?" We had a big wall map studded with tacks, so I looked over to the map and said, "There are your wagon routes, here is a list of the men who made the great increases. Here is their territory. This shows your increasing business as coming from the well-to-do, and the substantial families in

Cleveland." The executive turned to Hill and said, "Dave is right; we'll use them all."

The next day we were having a conference on some other matter. Neither Hill nor I could ever recall what we were talking about. Rothlesberger, the manager of the plant was with us and we were discussing some subject when we heard a moan at the door and we all gazed spellbound at a boy employee standing at the door crying and holding in one hand a part of his other hand which had been cut off by a machine. We were all shocked; the ambulance was called and the boy sent to the hospital, and when we assembled an hour later not one of us could think of what happened at our meeting. We talked this matter over and we decided that when there was any great news in the paper or anything very dramatic, the sinking of a great steamer or a statesman meeting the assassin's bullet or a great fire in the city, that we would never advertise, because advertising was only like a game of marbles, and no one watched the marble game when the fire engines were going by. We would not use the Sunday newspapers for the same reason; there was too much to attract the readers' attention. We picked out the light days, Tuesday, Wednesday and Thursday, when there was a slight lull in the business.

When it was announced that we had closed the campaign in Cleveland and were going to Chicago, the newspapers paid my company the greatest compliment that I believe has ever been paid any company. Each of the newspapers printed on their front page a cartoon. I have never seen anything like them in my forty years' experience. The Plain Dealer gave us 500 lines of cartoon by their artist top front page. It showed a picture of the City of Cleveland with its houses and factories and above them was the loaf of Ward's Tip-

AN IRISH BOY IN AMERICA 115

Top Bread with lines drawn around it showing the speed of the loaf. Old Mose Cleveland stood on the edge of the city and his words were, "My, that loaf of bread surely put this town in a swirl."

The World's cartoon was also on the front page, as were all the papers. There was a picture of a kitchen and on the table was a molding board and rolling pin covered with spider's web and the heading was "Ward's Tip-Top Bread put the rolling pin and the molding board out of business."

The Press submitted five or six but they were pictures rather than cartoons. This was a Scripp-McRae paper. I believe it is now Scripp-Howard paper of much circulation and much desired by the advertiser. I believe they printed the cartoon from the Anziger. This showed a Dutch oven; Mother Cleveland is about to put the loaves of bread in the oven when Mose, pointing to a sunrise of Ward's Tip-Top Bread, says, "Wait, mother, this gives promise of being better."

Before going to Chicago I went back to Pittsburgh so that the children might have the dog to play with in Chicago. The dog was named Bessie, a cocker spaniel. When the kennel keeper turned her over to me I never saw so much joy in my life. She was tickled pink. She jumped up and ran around me and barked and tried to kiss me. She had not seen me for six months and I know that if I could have interpreted her bark she would have said, "How is the rest of the family?" All the boys in Pittsburgh were in to see me and they told me that the campaign the Times had put on would never be forgotten. Ten years afterwards Mr. Mathews said to me, "Here is what I consider the greatest newspaper campaign ever put out." He pulled out of his pigeon hole the Times campaign. I said, "Why, Mr. Mathews, that is my campaign." "Well,

I knew you had been in Pittsburgh, but never connected the two. Let me congratulate you on this wonderful campaign."

After trying a boarding house for a while in Chicago, we were able to get a furnished house on Prairie Avenue which was the street on which Marshall Field lived. The newspaper specials all came to see me. They had heard about the Cleveland campaign. Montgomery of the Tribune introduced me to the publisher afterwards, a United States Senator, Medill McCormick. He said he wanted to meet the man who standardized bread through advertising. I explained of course that it was the company who did that and not myself. He gave me a desk in his office with Harry Parker, who was then advertising man.

Our campaign in Chicago was laid out on similar lines to that which had proved so successful in Cleveland. There were the letters to the dealers, better illustrations now and probably better set-ups. We ran all the newspaper teasers telling about the gold and silver thimbles lost in Chicago and these were illustrated by a picture of a very beautiful girl who was called Miss Chicago. Everything was lovely until the fourth day, when the big announcement in all the papers telling that Ward's bread the next day would have so many gold and so many silver thimbles. I believe we doubled the amount. That night we had all the newspaper men at the opening of the bakery.

The day of our triumph arrived. That is the day that Ward's bread containing the gold and silver thimbles was to be on sale. The bank was ready to redeem the thimbles on presentation. Ten dollars in gold for the finder of the gold thimble and five silver dollars for those who found the silver thimbles. And each one to keep his find as a souvenir of the bakers of Tip-Top Bread.

Then the bank telephoned. A mob with thimbles was besieging the bank. There were thousands of them and they all wanted the rewards. The bank had called the police and these men wanted the company to come and explain some things. This is what happened another bakery company put thimbles in every loaf of their bread that day. Our people got an injunction against them.

We appeared before Judge Landis now of baseball fame. He was trying the twenty-nine million dollar Rockefeller case and the judge had no time for little jobs like ours, so he assigned it to Judge Kohlsteat. I can see him now, sitting on his bench, a man of seventy-five years or more. Partly asleep as our lawyer began to unfold the story. As the tale went on, I watched the judge and he reminded me of Longfellow's launching of the ship: "She starts, she moves, she seems to feel the thrill of life along her keel." The judge jumped to his feet and said, "How dare you bring into my court a lottery." Biff, bang, we were out in the street.

Our campaign was suspended. Every morning I reported to the factory for about six weeks and every week my pay envelope would come along. During that time the factory was robbed three times, twice at night and once in the day time. A couple of fellows came in one noon with guns and held up the factory and took considerable stuff from the master baker's locker. I saw them walking out the door, revolvers in each hand. We notified the police and the next day at ten o'clock two detectives came in to see us.

Lawlessness was rampant in Chicago. Parker told me there were at least eighty highway robberies at night which the papers didn't publish as they didn't want strangers to be alarmed. They would not only take their valuables but also their clothes and leave them in the cold to perish. I admit that I have walked in the middle of the road on the way home nights and stayed home nearly every night. I afterwards became associated with the Hearst newspapers and in a hundred or more calls on business men in every case but two on the desk at the business man's right hand was a loaded revolver. I spoke to the two and asked them why it was. These men showed me that in their desks they also had guns. One street in Chicago, Halstead, had fifty-four saloons in a continuous row. There were 4,000 saloons and 2,000 police. Murder was frequent, but when a beautiful choir girl was murdered one night, public indignation compelled the reduction of the saloons to 2,000 and the increase of the police to 4,000. Police officials told me that in winter all the desperadoes come into Chicago from the West and that this is why there is so much crime. They also said that the elected judge who is under the thumb of the boss is the next greatest evil.

CHAPTER XI

R. B. Ward came over from Pittsburgh one day and told me of the wonderful campaign they would have in May when they would open the Boston plant. This was in March, and I said, "What are you going to do with me in the meantime?" He thought I might get a job. "Well," I said, "while there is no written contract there is an implied contract, and I think you ought to give me my pay until I get another job," so he agreed to give me four weeks' pay and as it was the middle of the week he would make an even check for $200. I said, "I will release you from any obligation, but in the meantime it will also release me from all obligation to the Wards and I don't have to go to Boston."

On the way home I dropped into a print shop, had a printer get out for me one hundred letters. In this letter I told my story, who I was, what I had done, and stated that I wanted a job. I received forty-four answers to call for an interview. One of these was from the "Fair," a big department store. They offered me a job as assistant advertising manager and would make me advertising manager if I only knew merchandise. I refused this and went with the Hearst newspapers in Chicago.

When I reported for work I was sent out on automobile row. They had never been able to get any automobile advertising and any representative they had sent out there had been kicked out of the establishments. "They didn't like them and you are a great breezy fellow," said the publisher. I was a six-footer, weighed 200 pounds and there were very few men who could kick me out.

Representing an unpopular daily newspaper is a hardship. When every call you make means a battle with the advertiser, life is not a rosy dream. Hearst was unpopular in Chicago at that time, at least with the automobile dealers.

Luckily the publisher who hired me for publicity manager thought it a good thing to turn me loose in automobile row and see for myself what the average attitude was toward the two Hearst daily newspapers. I had been out of work for a couple of weeks and now that I had a job, I meant to stick if I had to fight every man along automobile row. While I was big and strong, I had never hit a man in my life. A man in New York threatened to throw me out of a window in the fourteenth story of the Flat Iron building and I told him he could not do it; after looking me over he decided that it would not be wisdom to try.

This man was an advertising agent. He had the account of a Fifth Avenue perfumer and hit on the bright idea of using the perfume on the paper rolls from which the Minneapolis Tribune was printed. Starke wrote all the foreign advertisers about it and said that there were so many rotten and vile advertisements in the Tribune that all the perfume in the world would not kill the stench. Then he sent me to see the advertising agent to get the business for the Minneapolis Journal. When I told the good man I represented Starke, he saw red. He was the angriest man I ever saw. After our encounter I called on the perfumer and got a letter telling him to give me the business. This advertiser told me that he had just got word that his boy was in the South and was dying of pneumonia. I felt sorry for him and I do hope that his boy recovered.

I went back to the agency and presented the note and the agency man spent half an hour trying to get me to quit Starke and go to work for him.

My first call on automobile row was on the Cadillac dealer. He was talking to an employment agency and the talk was like this:

"Say, Bill, send me a secretary. Listen, boy, she must be a good looker. I don't care a damn whether she can spell or type, but I want her to look as good as the car; Bill, old boy, do this for me and I will send a car around Sunday afternoon for you and the family."

This man is human, I thought, and if the rest of them are like him I can get along. I made a lot of fine friends in automobile row. Hearst foreign service, of which Whitman was the head, covered the agencies while I covered the local houses. Whitman was very nice to me and he afterward become publisher of the Boston American, New York Commercial and the other day returned to the Hearst ranks and is publisher of the Atlanta Georgian. We had an auto show and I covered it. I think we had twenty-two auto ads in the Hearst papers in the show number.

The Pierce-Arrow man said to me one day, "Would you mind having the paper bill me for that advertising I gave you instead of sending the bill to Buffalo?"

I said, "Sure, but why?"

He said that he had General Pierce and other officials of the factory at dinner at his house and they all sure jumped on the Hearst publications.

"I know the arguments you gave me but somehow or another they didn't seem to be the way you gave them to me and I decided I would pay those bills myself."

I said, "Don't be a dummy; send on the bills." He told me an interesting story with a good moral. One day a man came in and bought a Pierce Arrow. In giving his name and address he turned out to be Marshall Field, so he said, "Mr. Field, you will want more than one auto. You surely can use four or five; why not let me be of service to you?" Field said no, but came back in a month and ordered five more cars. He said, "You know, I run a store but I don't know about autos, so I went to New York where I was unknown and I saw four or five of the best autos. I would say to the salesman, 'I grant you are the best, but what is the next best?' The whole half dozen said Pierce Arrow was second best, so I came back to you." Since that time I never have told an advertiser what was the second best proposition.

When I first met Paulman of the Pierce Arrow Company, he complained of a sore throat. He had been to a specialist and it was not better. He was worried as most sick men are. I told him my mother had used a local remedy for sore throat for all her children for more than fifty years and the results had always been satisfactory. Paulman sent to Fall River and got a bottle and in a few days he was a very grateful man. That is what got me the Pierce Arrow business. I find if you do most men a kindness they will sit up nights until they get square with you. I have great faith in the good of humanity.

When Paulman learned I was going back to Boston he told me he had me picked out for manager of his commercial department of the Pierce Arrow and that he would send a Pierce Arrow around to the house the morning before my departure so we would see the entire city.

I was enjoying Chicago very much. There was

something doing every minute. I was getting fifty dollars a week and a chance for one hundred dollars. One day I got a wire to call Ward Baking Company up at eight o'clock at night in Pittsburgh.

They agreed to give $50 a week, a year's contract and $250 travelling expenses. The money came the next day and in a few days I was in Pittsburgh.

I was shown the plan of campaign in Pittsburgh. It was clever, I think the cleverest thing I have ever seen. The plan was to advertise that the Ward Company had a label on their bread and if the buyer would bring to their factory label No. 1144, he would get ten dollars in gold, but this bread had been baked three days before and was no longer on sale.

The thought behind this campaign was that after these advertisements had been printed three or four times the customer would buy the bread in anticipation of the future offerings of the company. I wired my family to come on from Chicago and met them at Youngstown, so the Lawlors came back to the East after two years' absence.

R. B. Ward, the President of the Company, came back with us. We were sitting out on the promenade deck on one of the steamers of the Fall River Line, and as we were sailing down the Sound I pointed over to New York and said, "There is where you ought to have a bakery." "I am afraid of New York, Dave," he said, "it is too big." They have a magnificent bakery at the very spot I pointed out and another in Brooklyn now. R. B. like the rest of us got courage with the years. Today the Ward Baking Company has twenty-one bakeries and a capital of $44,000,000. R. B. said, "Dave, did I ever tell you how I got in the bakery business? I will tell you and Mrs. Lawlor.

"When I was a young man I was a clerk in a grocery

store in Allegheny City. One day a man came in the store. He was a phrenologist and wanted to examine my head. I asked if it would hurt and how much it would be. He told me it wouldn't hurt and it would cost me twenty-five cents. After the examination he said, 'Young man, you have a fine head on you; you should go into business.' I smiled and said, 'What business?' He said, 'You would be a success in most any line of business, but you ought to go into the bakery business.'

"That evening on the way to see the girl whom I afterwards had the good fortune to marry I saw a sign in a bakery window 'For Sale.' I went in and had a chat with the owner of the business and in the evening I told my girl about my talk with the Phrenologist, that on my way to her house I had seen this bake shop advertised for sale, and that the owner told me the price was three hundred dollars. She jumped up and said, 'Robert, buy it, buy it!' I said, 'My dear, all I have in the world is four hundred dollars, and we are going to be married in a week.' She said, 'You buy it and we will get married on one hundred dollars. You bake and I will take care of the front store.'"

That, he said, was the beginning of the Ward Baking Company.

You won't find this story in the books on the Ward Baking Company's success, but this is the story as told to Mary and me by Robert Boyd Ward. I never saw him when he was not cheery. Let me tell this little story here: Years afterward, he bought the Federal League Baseball team in Brooklyn. Mary and I and the boy were often his guests in the private box. One day he called me from my wife's side and we sat apart from the others. He said, "Dave, I have lost $700,000 on this ball park. This is the only venture I ever made without consulting my wife. She has never been to see a ball game and she won't come. I have finally persuaded my daughters to come, but the day I get my good wife to sit in that box I will forget the $700,000 loss. I think far more of my wife's wishes and affection than I do any amount of money."

We had our furniture brought from the warehouse in Providence and we soon had a beautiful apartment on Vincent Street in Cambridge. The campaign opened on May 1st, 1906. There was a half-page advertisement in every Boston, Providence, Pittsburgh, Cleveland and Chicago paper, same copy running in all cities. Every grocery dealer in all these cities received the letters and the samples of bread as outlined in the Cleveland campaign. The newspapers all sent their reporters for a story of the plant and its product.

I met all the Boston newspaper boys and told them I was going to make an address to the thousands who had been invited to the opening but it would not be necessary for them to make a note as I was giving each of them a story of the plant and its product, how bread was made and how Ward's bread differed from any other bread.

In this way I avoided a garbled story and all the newspapers gave wonderful space to this new loaf of bread, and 'twas a great loaf of bread.

Among those who came to us that day was a flour man and he said, "Now, Mr. Lawlor, that was a great advertisement in the paper, but don't you think you went too far?" I asked him in what way. "Why," he said, "you claim it is the greatest loaf of bread in the world." "Isn't it?" "Why, yes, but you might at least be modest about it," he answered. I said, "My good man, the advertising this morning cost us over $2,000. Were we not justified in saying we have the greatest loaf of bread in the world when we have it? Why do you suppose we buy space? Is it to tell people our bread is as good as somebody else's?" "I guess you are right, I never looked at it that way," he said.

After the sixth advertisement which appeared, we introduced a little corner piece reading, "Warning—things are not what they seem; did you look for the red, white and blue label on Ward's bread when you purchased it? We printed on the labels three days ago a series of numbers. This bread has been withdrawn from the market but if you have kept No. 41144677 and No. 41144678 we will give you a ten-dollar gold piece for these labels." Of course the thought was to bring to the housewives a feeling of regret that she had not saved the labels and bring to her mind the thought that there might be more prizes offered. Every other day these labels would be printed and the sales began to increase. The campaign was stopped in Pittsburgh after the fifteenth issue and in Chicago the next day. In Providence and Boston not until we reached the thirty-second piece of copy. Then I got a call from the Boston postmaster and I went to see him. We were accused of running a lottery and I showed him just one copy of the advertisement and this showed the bread had been removed from sale before the offer was made. He said that he couldn't see any lottery to it but it would be reported to Washington. I assured him that was the last piece of copy as we didn't want the matter to have to go to Washington. I continued the copy without this warning, but I had small posters made and put them in our five thousand groceries that handled our bread. These posters had the winning numbers for which we would give ten dollars.

One day I got a phone call—"This Mr. Lawlor?"

"Yes, sir." "This is the Chief of the State Police." "Good morning, Chief." "You're running a lottery and I want it stopped."

"But it is not a lottery, Chief," I assured him.

"Well, you stop or will I come over and pinch you?" he bellowed.

"Chief, it will stop," I replied meekly.

We had in addition to the letters, newspapers and posters, wagon loads of bread going around the various neighborhoods. Pretty girls went from door to door and asked housewives to try it. Sales went up leaps and bounds. They tell me the factory went on dividend basis in three weeks. In eight weeks we had spent about $32,000, and as we had selected the light days when there was very little advertising our campaign made a great impression on the public. Every day we had the salesmen assemble and gave them what is now known as ginger talks. I made all these talks to the men and they became very fond of me.

If any man fell down or was out on account of taking a drink too much, he and I had a private chat and he always left me with a promise to do better. I don't know how it came about, but R. B. Ward knew of every one of these talks and he said that he knew the success of the bakery was in a measure due to my work. Then he said, "Dave, advertising is certainly wonderful; in three weeks you have put this bakery in sales where it took me fifteen years in Pittsburgh to get that same volume, and in six months here you have put this bakery where it has taken me twenty-five years. I never knew that advertising was such a wonderful power."

Every night we brought a couple of hundred people through the bakery. This work I assumed and we began at where the flour came in and followed the bread through to the finished loaf, and then handed them a couple of loaves to take home with them.

When I was in Cambridge about ten days my two little boys were playing in the yard when another little boy came over to see them. He had broken quarantine as he was isolated on account of having scarlet fever. My boys were friendly little fellows and they played with him for an hour or two. A day or two afterwards the eldest boy, Paul, became ill and I called in the doctor; finally they told me the boy had scarlet fever, and the next day David showed that he had it. In two or three days Mary and I knelt by his bedside and saw Paul go back to God from Whom he had come. He died early in the morning and at three o'clock in this strange city I went looking for an undertaker. They told me the funeral would have to be private so I took his little body and the casket back to Fall River. The body was put on the driver's seat and we started along for the cemetery. I saw my brother John and his good wife. They didn't dare come any nearer for they had children and they were afraid of scarlet fever. This little boy now sleeps all alone in the lot on a corner plot.

The editor of the Herald used to come to see us and the children used to romp around and beg him for a story. He would exclaim, "My Lord, Dave, where did you get them? Such wondrous love I have never seen." I always put them to bed and told them stories until they fell asleep.

I did many things that were for the good of the company. I sold what is called the "stale" to many institutions and I sold several of the larger restaurants. One day George Bollinger, sales manager, said, "Dave, there is a place over in the city called Thompson's Spa;

there is nothing like it in this country. The furnishings are gorgeous and the fifty women waitresses are all beauties. They sell food to about 40,000 people a day of the highest class. This lunch room gets its rolls from Philadelphia twice a day. Every baker in town is trying to sell them but they refuse to buy from a local bakery. They feel that the advertisement they get in having their rolls come from Philadelphia is a great advertisement for them. We have had our salesman and even our superintendent of sales over to see them but they won't even give them audience. You can sell them and I wish you would do this." "George," I said, "I don't believe that any man goes to Philadelphia for rolls that he can get here. They must be a higher quality than anything that is manufactured here, but I will sell them." The master baker of all the bakeries, John Tally, was in town and we went to Thompson's and had coffee and rolls, and I asked him if he could bake one better. He said, "Sure," and he baked fifty for me that night, but I told him that they were not as good.

The local master baker, Henry Engel, and I went over to Thompson's every night for two weeks and sat on the stools, drank their coffee, ate their rolls and every night he would bake fifty rolls which I found fault with and threw in the scrap heap. At the end of two weeks Henry had produced a roll that looked very good to me and I said, "Now you are getting somewhere. I will go over to see Mr. Eaton and the first thing he will do is to cut it." The first one I cut was full of yeast holes. It took this great baker, with all his knowledge of baking, two weeks more to make a perfect roll. I said, "I will sell this roll to Eaton, Henry, but I would like to compare it with their roll, so I sent one of the men over to get some unbuttered rolls. He was from the South and called every girl he met "Sister," a habit he transferred to me. He came back with buttered rolls and said he had talked with a very nice young lady and he told her he was on a journey and wanted half a dozen unbuttered rolls and that butter made him ill. He had not eaten a buttered roll in twenty years on the advice of his physician. The young lady talked with the office and said, "I am sorry, but you will have to take the buttered rolls or go without." I could have buttered our rolls but we never had an ounce of butter in the bake shop. We used cotton seed oil. Butter became rancid under heat of 400 degrees, while the cotton seed oil could stand that amount of heat. I slit the rolls and put on a drop of cotton seed oil and they came out delicious. Every one laughed and I wondered if that was the reason that we couldn't get an unbuttered roll.

I telephoned Mr. Eaton for an appointment and met him within an hour with a suitcase of bread and rolls. I complimented him on the beauty of his place, the excellence of his food and above all in the classy waitresses whom he employed.

He told me that he had a gang of painters go over the place every night so that it was prepared to open new every morning, that the food was the best he could get and prepared by able chefs. He said the girls all had not only to be good to look at, but every one of them had to be a woman of refinement; in fact each had to show by her way she was to the manner born.

Eaton admired the rolls, spoke of our wonderful newspaper campaign and said we must be real people. He told me that he would have to submit my rolls to a special process and I assured him he would find them all right, as I had submitted them to his special process before I brought them over. He looked surprised but made no comment. In the afternoon he phoned and asked me the price. I gave our regular price plus expressage from Philadelphia. He asked if the price was not high, and I countered by asking him if he did not want the best roll made. Then he asked me to send him two hundred rolls; in a few days this was increased to four hundred, then eight hundred and finally to eighteen hundred, which was then the total consumption.

Ward still supplies these rolls to Thompson and I figured the other day that this sale has brought Ward more than $150,000. R. B. came over shortly after I made the sale and asked me what I was getting for the rolls and I told him. He slapped me on the back and said, "Dave, you're a wonder."

Some years afterward I met Archibald, the general manager of Thompson's Spa. He said he was on vacation when we made the deal with Eaton, and he was the most surprised man in town when he found we had an even better roll than that they got from Philadelphia.

Then he told me that years before they got tired of buying from Philadelphia. Trains would be late or delayed, so they got the formula and gave it to Fox and Ferguson, the two big Boston bakeries. The product from each was unsatisfactory, so they sent to Philadelphia and hired the man who made the rolls and put him in Ferguson's Bakery. They got more poor rolls and the baker said there was something the matter with the water or the air of Boston, that a good roll could never be baked here, and we, by George, the first crack out of the box made a far better roll than ever came out of Philadelphia. So after all it is the product and not the salesman that makes the sale. When both are good so much the better, but many a lame duck of a salesman is being carried along by the excellence of his product, while many a good salesman is sick at heart because his product does not measure up. This is true also of the newspaper, which is simply a product like bread or shoes or soap. Some publishers who fail to make a good product, like some manufacturers who make an inferior article, are looking for some sales manager of salesmen who can perform miracles.

CHAPTER XII

At the end of eight months I was asked to report in Cleveland. I wrote, regretting the fact that I would be unable to go, that I was going to stay in Boston and asked them to kindly send me my bonus as agreed. R. B. Ward came on to see me and said, "What are your plans, Dave?" I said, "I am going on the Boston Herald." He put his arms around my neck and said, "Dave, you are a man of wonderful ability and I am sorry we have nothing big enough to give you, but if you ever need a friend, come to me and you will find what friendship is." So I left the Wards and went to work on the Herald. Twice afterward the Wards came to me and I handled their campaign with my other work, but this story will be told in its place.

Haskell of the Boston Herald hired me at fifty dollars per week as an advertising solicitor. He gave me the promise that if I was the man he thought I was at the end of three or six months he would make me advertising manager. He introduced me to the business manager, and he asked him to give me a list of accounts. This man had been an advertising agent and made a lot of money in advertising Paine's Celery Compound and Diamond Dyes. He was a friend of Haskell and put some money into the business, so he was some power there. At that time he was a haughty, arrogant man; today he is much humbler and friendlier. We often chat together at the club.

He gave me a list of men who had been out of the paper for three years or more. It was a very fine list of names; in fact he confessed to me in later years that he had his own staff of men and he could not afford to have a new man come in and make any show, but he said, "I don't mind telling you now that you were the ablest advertising man that ever stepped into the Herald." This game of giving a salesman a dead list is the favorite way of getting rid of a man in any organization.

The boss sends a man with instructions to give him a chance. He is given a list of dead ones and the boss is shown the results. "They like the young fellow but he is out of his element, too quiet, too refined, not roughneck enough for the business." I remember the first call I made was on a wholesale liquor dealer on Federal Street. I told him I was from the Herald, that we missed his advertising, and that Mr. Haskell had sent me down to see just what the trouble was. He asked me to sit down and rang for his bookkeeper to bring the records. Then he explained to me that he sold by mail four quarts of whiskey for three dollars. This was the text of his advertising and then he showed me the results from advertising.

The cost of selling three dollars worth of whiskey from the Post was $7.00. The Globe cost $8.00 and the American $9.00, the Journal $12.00 and the Herald $84.00. He said, "I am willing to pay as high as $12.00 to sell three dollars worth of whiskey, because the repeat orders would show me a profit, but I cannot spend $84.00. What have you got to say about that?" I said, "You believe the Herald has readers?" He said, "Yes, I read it myself." I said, "I think, Mr. Callahan, you are a poor salesman. When they read your advertising in the other papers they say to themselves, 'Some cheap little Irish rumseller on Federal Street,' and dismiss you from their thoughts without knowing the quality you handle. Get a page ad in the Herald and show the whole building and the various activities of the establishment and tell the story of your place." He said, "What will that ad cost me?" I told him "About $720," to which he replied, "All right, have your artist come down and make a picture and you write the copy."

I don't know what the matter was with the Herald Advertising Department, but it took them nearly three months to get the job finished. About every day Stevens would ask me about Callahan. You know a drop of water dropped on the head in the same place a sufficient number of times is apt to kill a man but I was always courteous to him. One day the job was finished and we took it down to Callahan and he said, "Beautiful, but I cannot give you an order for it today. My brother and I have had a disagreement and it has come to the point of buying or selling. I am going to buy. If he saw this advertisement I would have to pay $50,000 more for the business, but you wait a month or six weeks and I will give you that order."

I often asked for some live accounts, but was always refused. I did get some of the list in, Washburn Credit, Dodge Sport Department Store and Brine's Department Store. The first advertisement I got for the Herald was from Henry Brine. He was always nice to me from the first day down to now; he has a smile for me that warms the cockles of my heart.

There was one firm, Gale and Kent, still in business, who were very friendly to me and at the end of five months Kent asked if he could talk with the publisher; so he called Haskell on the phone and asked for an appointment. Just what Haskell said I don't know, but Kent said, "I know you have an advertising department, why one of your men has been here every day for five months. We expect him out to the house soon. He showed a circulation statement which we believe a lie."

Kent said, "Your Mr. Lawlor showed your circulation and he has sold us on the idea of the paper. We don't believe you have that circulation and we think you are not telling the truth. We spend $20,000 a year in advertising and we will give you $15,000 of it if you will show us 125,000 circulation, or just show us 100,000 circulation of the Herald. We don't believe you have it." Mr. Haskell hemmed and hawed, and Kent said, "Just show me 90,000 and you can have the business," but Mr. Haskell would not show it, for the Herald didn't have it.

A few days afterward the manager told me that he was sorry, but that Haskell had ordered my dismissal. He tells me now, more than twenty years afterward, that Haskell had often asked for my dismissal, but he had refused because I was too good a man to let go. I suppose Haskell was hungry for business and he didn't see me getting it, but did see the fifty dollars on the payroll. He did not have wit enough to have a talk with me, but went on the face of the returns. Nowadays some good organizations do not let a man go until the boss has a talk with him. This prevents department heads doing certain things detrimental to the interest of the house.

While I was on the Herald I was introduced to Don Seitz of the World. We rode to Providence together and he offered me a job on the World, but I refused. I told him I knew I would get fired from the Herald but I was no quitter. He said when that happened he would have a place for me in the World.

So I went to the World office and asked for him. Tommy Croft, the advertising manager, asked me what

I wanted to see Mr. Seitz about. I told him of the promise and he excused himself to see Mr. Seitz, but returned with the message that he had nothing for me nor did he care to see me.

I saw the manager of the Hearst foreign department and he hired me at forty dollars a week. I had a rooming house on 84th Street and lived on a lenten diet because I had a family to support in Boston. We got an apartment on Broadway and 136th Street, four rooms and bath, forty dollars. At that time my boy was about three years old and he and Mary spent their time on the Riverside Drive, which was just being built.

The fresh air from the Hudson soon brought the bloom to both their cheeks and we were very happy. One day half a dozen of us were discharged. One of the men was Miller, who afterward became New England manager of N. W. Ayer. Every time he would see me for some years he would say, "Dave, remember the day we were fired from the Hearst organization for being no good?" Neither of us had a chance; there were about twenty men on the staff and the man who gave out the assignments saw to it that Miller would get a small ad in Newark to chase, while mine would be a want ad on Staten Island. Billy Freeman then put me on the staff of the American. This was the morning paper and the first venture of Hearst in New York. It was established about thirty-five years ago and was also considered a weak sister. I told Freeman one day what I thought about the paper and he asked me if I wouldn't see Brad Merrill, the publisher. I did, and spent two hours with him telling him what was wrong with the American and what should be done. He was nice, courteous and cold, and he stayed there for more than twenty years afterward, but never made a change, so it is still a weak sister.

My job was to put on a 125th Street edition, so I went from store to store and made daily reports to Freeman. I was quite successful. Freeman used to bring me to his house and introduced me to his wife, son and daughter. He was a very able man and I was very fond of him. Hearst paid him $25,000 a year and he lived at the rate of $35,000; I understand that Hearst paid his bills two or three times, but the final break came. Billy Freeman was a great advertising man, great salesman and great man—were he Scotch and saved his money he would have been a millionaire, but then probably he would not have been the able advertising man that he was. My job was completed during the bank-run.

The Knickerbocker bank got into trouble and a run started. The line at the 125th Street bank must have been a quarter of a mile long. People stood there in line from nine o'clock until three, drawing out their money, and about everyone who drew it out took it to the bank across the street. I have forgotten the name of the bank, but Montgomery was the president of it, so there was almost as big a line putting in money. That night the Knickerbocker failed and in the morning Montgomery's bank failed and the next day there was a run on fully one hundred banks in New York. It was hard to get money. Manufacturers could not pay their help and nobody paid a newspaper. Saturday night twenty advertising men on the American were discharged, and I was one of the twenty. There was no two weeks' pay for gratuity, just thrown right out on a cold, cruel world. We had an indignation meeting in front of the office which was down in front of City Hall Park. One of the men discharged was a brother-in-law of Peter Butler, who had hundreds of stores in New York. He was a surgeon with the rank of major in Egypt under Roberts and Kitchener, and left the service for some reason or other. Butler got Freeman to put him on the advertising staff. Billy said he put him on just to show New York what a real gentleman was. He was a scholarly Irish gentleman. He wore spats, a monocle and carried a cane. He really was well groomed and you would look twice at him—a woman would probably look three times. He took charge of the meeting and said, "Boys, I am really glad it happened, because you know Mr. Freeman told me to keep after copy for a Christmas issue and to start at 23rd Street up to Times Square and then upon the other side. The reception I got was terrible. Some of them held their noses and some of them thumbed their noses. I was harassed in mind and spirit and I went home one night during the week sick of the business. I wouldn't eat supper but my good wife insisted I should, so after supper I went to bed, but couldn't sleep, so I got up and began to make the rounds again. Finally I went to one office and a gentleman smiled and said, 'Hearst's American?' and I thought he went after writing materials. Suddenly I heard a commotion at the door and my friend was pointing his finger at me. Beside him were four thugs and this supposed friend said, 'There is one of Hearst's minions, grab him!' They dragged me to the twelfth floor and over to the elevator well. They put a rope around my neck and threw me down the shaft. I would have been dashed to pieces, but the rope nearly strangled me and I woke up." We all laughed, and the meeting was over.

The panic caused by the failure of the banks seemed to make it impossible to get a job. I made many calls but it was the same story everywhere. The selling forces had been reduced to a minimum. I was down to the last dollar. Blue? Not for a moment, not, in fact, for a moment in my whole life. I always believed that He who looked after the birds of the air would take care of me and He did. I got a wire from Frank Callahan that he was ready to run the page that I had planned and he was sending fifty dollars for me to come over to see him. I left thirty-five dollars in the house and made the trip on fifteen dollars. Frank Callahan said, "This is a wonderful advertisement and we will use every paper in town except the Herald on account of the way they used you." I said, "No, Frank, the Herald first; it was sold to you on Herald time." The Herald got the first page, then the Globe, Post, Journal and American. I wrote a series of ten seventy-line advertisements for follow-ups. There was a monogram of the J. F. Callahan Company, then a human nature talk on who pays for the license, the lights and the bartender's smile, and the advertising showed you could buy for three and a half cents from Frank Callahan what you paid fifteen cents for when you put your elbow on the bar and your foot on the rail. Frank told me some weeks afterward that this copy produced wonderful results until one day his twenty retailers came in a bunch and told him that he would either quit this style of advertising or they would withdraw their business, and as he could not afford to lose the wholesalers he quit. Frank has gone on, but I believe I never met a kindlier man. He was a college man, refined and intelligent. He inherited this business from his father and found it $125,000 in debt. In a few years he paid off the indebtedness and was making a great deal of money. He saw prohibition coming and got rid of his stock of goods. Many of the wholesalers believed it was a joke so they put their goods in storage, but they have been paying storage charges all these years.

I went back to New York and the thirty-five dollars soon melted away, so we were again down to the last dollar. Among the places I visited when looking for work was the Beckwith Special Agency. There I met James Tripp Beckwith, who was the head then of this great special agency. His brother Sam had represented us when I was advertising manager of the Providence News. Mr. Beckwith was very sympathetic, but had no place for me. I suggested that he ought to have a paper in Boston and I would go and look the field over and make a report to him on the situation for fifty dollars. He gave me the fifty dollars, so I left thirty-five dollars at home again and with the fifteen dollars made a trip to Boston. I met A. E. Sproule on the street. He was one of the men from the advertising agency that I covered when I was on the Fall River Globe.

The first time I met Sproule and told him I was from the Globe, he showed me the Globe folder and in it was a memorandum signed by himself never to do any business with the Globe under any conditions. I straightened out this matter and we became very friendly. I dropped into the Boston American and there I met Capt. W. J. DeVinney, who was assistant advertising manager. When I brought the Ward campaign to Boston I had all the copy set up in that office. DeVinney was quite helpful in its preparation. He was a New Hampshire man of Irish parentage, studied law, enlisted in the Spanish-American War as a private and came out with the rank of captain. He was one of the handsomest men I ever saw. He inquired about New York and I told him I was out of work over there. He said that my attire didn't look very good and I ought to have a new hat and shoes, that employers noticed appearances. I agreed but told him I was broke. He said, "Wait a minute," and gave me twenty dollars, and from that moment began a lifetime friendship with DeVinney. I made my report to Beckwith. I told him I had visited the four papers and selected one that I thought he could get.

When I reached home I found a telegram from Sproule urging me to come to Boston as advertising manager for Fibre and Fabric, a textile paper which he had recently purchased. He offered me forty dollars a week. I told Mary that while I was very fond of New York it was better to work for forty dollars in Boston than to loaf in New York, and when the panic was over we would go back again to the grand city.

It was about five degrees below zero on the morning I started to work on Fibre and Fabric. I worked most of the day and in the afternoon I made a call that required a trip on the tunnel cars of the Boston Elevated. I rode in the smoker, and as there were no seats I had to hang onto a strap. Some other good fellow stood behind me with his cigar in his hand and burned a beautiful hole in the back of my overcoat. It was really a handsome hole, two inches in diameter, and very well done. I went into Gale and Kent to have it repaired. These were the boys I solicited every day on the Herald. While having the coat repaired Kent said, "Dave, you ought to have some new clothes. You are a brilliant man and ought to dress befitting your station in life." I explained that I was broke and Kent said, "Well, this is a cash business, but let me make you two suits of clothes. If you ever get the money pay me; if you don't, we'll never send you a bill." This led to a good friendship with these two fine gentlemen that has lasted nearly thirty years, and I hope will last through life.

Kent is a Southerner, born in Atlanta, Georgia. He is a wonderful character. He is not a churchgoer, but very charitable. I know that he has spent $35,000 educating six young men. He put them all through college and saw that they got a good start in life, but he will swear. He is very proficient at it. Many times I have spoken about it to him, and he said once that riding on the train from Washington to New York the only seat that could be had was with a Catholic priest. He told the priest he had a friend in Boston who often came in to see him and this friend interrupted him and said one day, "Kent, listen, I am a member of the Holy Name Society and every time you swear I must make an act of reparation for your sin. I am now eighty-six acts behind. So at least shut up until I square my account."

When the first day's work was done on Fibre and Fabric I had to find a room at a modest price and I started out on my quest shortly after five o'clock, going from lodging house to lodging house until I could find a room at three dollars per week. That night it was fifteen degrees below zero. I had no cap and very tender ears, so every few moments I had to stop to warm my ears. I found a rooming house and stayed there for a couple of weeks, but then found a beautiful apartment on Beacon Street, Brookline, which had been erected that summer but not rented. I think the landlord liked my looks, because he offered me two months' rent free and a year's lease at sixty dollars a month. Mary and her sisters and the children arrived and we had a bowl of soup at the South Station. I asked her when the dining room furniture was coming but she said it was not coming—that the morning she was to leave the big city two of the Little Sisters of the Poor came in and asked for a donation. She gave them a cup of tea and said she didn't have any money to give them but if they would care to take a couple of beds, a few chairs and tables she would be delighted to do something for them. They were pleased. She asked them if they could get a man to move the furniture. They said they would move it themselves and the two Sisters and the boy who drove their wagon took the furniture. I laughed. She said, "You know they are doing wonderful work and we will get some new furniture."

When I went from Boston to New York I placed one-half the furniture in storage, so this was brought into the new house. Mary said the next day, "I have got to have some money." I asked her how much and she told me about a hundred dollars. I said, "All right, I will give you a hundred dollars tomorrow." She asked me where I would get it and I said I would write a story that night and sell it the next day for a hundred and twenty-five dollars. So I wrote the story on Home and the next day I dropped into Mathews' office and had it typed. I met Julius Mathews in the days when I solicited for the Fall River Globe, so he was glad to do this for me. At noon time I sold it to the Morse Furniture Company for a hundred and twenty-five dollars.

Mary was delighted—"Now write another story tonight and make another hundred dollars," she said. I was not very well that night, so I lay on the lounge and dictated a story of a piano to Mary and the next day Mathews' office again typed this story for me. I went down to the Chickering Piano Company and met the manager, who is now an official of the American

Piano Company. I told him I was a free lance writer and I had written a story about a piano which I wished him to look at. He sat over in the corner and said, "That is the finest thing in the English lauguage that was ever written about a piano. I will have to take the matter up with the head of the concern." Chickering bought this story.

A few weeks later Mary had to have another hundred dollars for the house and the night before I had been reading Hudson's "Psychic Phenomena." In this great book Hudson was telling about the great power of suggestion and to illustrate his point he took an apple pie, which many people thought caused indigestion. Hudson showed that no one could be healthy, happy and wise unless he started out in the morning with a piece of apple pie under his belt. I sold this story to Ernest Goulston, who was head of an advertising agency which was then handling the account of the Fox Bakery, and is now known as the "afternoon mayor of Boston." He gave me a hundred dollars for the right to publish this chapter of Hudson's copyrighted book. I wrote to the publisher and explained I was an advertising man and was delighted with Hudson's story of apple pie and asked for the privilege of publishing this chapter, which they granted. Fox Bakery sent out a million or two copies of this booklet. It was printed on alternate pages and the other carried the story of Smax Pie so it would look as though Hudson had Smax pie in mind. I afterwards bought books on Psychic Phenomena to give to my friends, but I could never find the story in subsequent editions.

CHAPTER XIII

I believe I was on Fibre and Fabric about six months, until changed conditions in the mill business put Fibre and Fabric on the rocks. The big asset of this concern was an employment department for mill overseers or superintendents. Wade, the former owner, knew all the mill owners and knew nearly all those who were looking for situations in mills. Sproule didn't have this knowledge, so lost the great income coming from this department.

I was out of a job again and I began negotiations with John H. Fahey, publisher of the Boston Traveler. This gentleman was afterwards president of the Boston Chamber of Commerce and president of all the Chambers of Commerce in the United States. The French government made him a chevalier in the Legion of Honor. He now owns the Worcester Post, which gives him a profit of about $75,000, and he has other interests that make him a rich man. He is now head of the Home Loan, Washington, D. C. In his office was a Mr. Benjamin Joy, a young man representing Gaston who was very much interested in the Traveler. He was at several interviews I had with Mr. Fahey. The publisher asked me what business I could get for the Traveler and I explained that that all depended on his work, that advertising began in the publisher's office, then was continued in the editorial, repertorial and circulation departments. In other words it depended on the product given the advertising man to sell.

Julius Mathews engaged me as a member of his staff. I had met Mr. Mathews one day on the street and talked about his papers. I believe he had about eighteen or twenty small papers at the time. I asked him why he didn't get some of the big business and explained to him that the reason men didn't do more was because they didn't attempt more. The next day he asked me to go to work for him. He said he had been offered the representation of Printers Ink and he would take it if I would agree to do all the work on it. All he could afford to give me was twenty-five dollars a week, but he would share fifty-fifty with me on anything that came into my department. Mathews looked good to me and I accepted his proposition.

It was Christmas Eve and he told me it had always been his custom to give to his employees a $2.50 gold piece, and now that I was a member of his staff his first act would be to give me the gold piece. On my way home that night I got off the car, bought a Christmas tree for my boy and lugged it home on my back and the whole $2.50 was spent on the tree for decorations and presents. That was twenty-seven years ago, and this friendship between Julius Mathews and myself exists today.

In all the years I was actively with Julius Mathews —more than fourteen years—he was always kind to me; there was never a harsh word or even a rising inflection of his voice. He is a great executive and a very kindly man. Of course he knew I couldn't live on the twenty-five dollars, and made an arrangement with the bookkeeper to give me anything I asked for. Once I was twelve hundred dollars in debt to him. He loaned me thirty-six hundred dollars to buy the house I live in. One year he gave me a check for two hundred and fifty dollars and said that was my dividend on the business. During those years in addition to my work on Printers Ink I was press agent to Storrow when he ran for mayor. Storrow paid me two hundred dollars a week for six weeks. I received fifty dollars a week for some years and gave him half of it from John Donnelly. The Boston Herald paid me one day forty-five hundred dollars for a contract I had with the Traveler of which I gave Mr. Mathews twenty-two hundred and fifty dollars. The Pilot at that time paid me about five thousand dollars, of which I gave Mr. Mathews one-half. Ben Joy of the Traveler had me write ten letters, for which he paid me two hundred and fifty dollars, and I wrote a series of letters for the Shawmut Bank, and also some interviews for which I received about six hundred dollars, one-half of which went to the agency.

For fourteen years we represented Printers Ink. We worked intelligently and faithfully and put a great deal of business into their Journal. Our arrangement with them was a twenty-five per cent commission. They had no business in New England and for the first year or two we lost money, but we did build the New England business up to about forty-five thousand dollars. I think that was about the last year we represented them, some fourteen years ago. In my travels I met nearly every publisher in New England and of course all advertisers whose business would be suitable for the problems of that Journal. New England advertising in Printers Ink, which was then owned by Romer and Lawrence, led the publishers from other parts of the country to seek its advertising columns.

Then in Printers Ink office Mr. Mathews was the great Mr. Mathews and I was the wonderful Mr. Lawlor. They reduced our commission to twenty per cent and then fifteen per cent and finally to ten per cent;

then they threatened to take away the representation unless we would accept the salary of sixty dollars a week. When they put on a monthly they increased this fifteen dollars a week and for this amount we were supposed to cover the whole of New England. Our reward after fourteen years of faithful effort was a notice that they would discontinue our service. Printers Ink is a great journal on advertising and anyone in the advertising business who does not read it misses something of value in its columns. John Irving Romer was a great editor; he often wondered why Mr. Mathews did not accept his invitations to lunch.

In the early years I sold a two-page spread to Comfort. This Gannett ran for some years. He met the raise in rates several times, but once he rebelled and refused to pay. He talked with Hopkins and Romer in New York about the advance and said he would not pay the price. They offered him page fourteen and fifteen at the same price, maintaining it was as good as the double center spread. Gannett refused to do business with them. The home office wired me that Gannett was to stop at the Hotel Erickson and for me to see him. I had dinner with this fine old gentleman and his family. He took me to a side room and after I stated my business he said, "You can't tell me that page fourteen and fifteen are as good as double center spread." I told him I didn't believe it was as good. He said, "Why are you here?" I told him I would tell him a story. I told him about a young man from Maine who became director in a Philadelphia bank, and after the meeting was over the old directors said that this man was all right in a country town bank and maybe in ten or fifteen years he would know something about city finance. The next week they found that this young man had purchased the majority of stock in the bank and they were working for him; the next week they found, to their amazement, that he had the majority of stock in the bank across the street, uniting the two banks. This was their dream for years, but they couldn't make any headway.

The Philadelphia Bulletin rushed a reporter to interview this new Napoleon of finance and asked him how he did it. He said it was the simplest thing in the world. All you had to do was know what you want, pay the price and take it. I said, "Gannett, you know what you want, why don't you pay the price and take it?" He said, "Wire the home office not to sell that space until they hear from me. Two days later from Augusta he wired to hold this for him at the new price. He occupied this position in Printers Ink for many years and it probably had much to do with making Comfort the great mail order Journal that it is. I don't know whether Gannett ever told this story to his son, but his son bought a daily newspaper in Portland, looked longingly at the Portland Express, the great newspaper there. He engaged Mr. Mathews to conduct negotiations, pay to them their price and combine the two papers. Mr. Mathews represents these papers in Portland and I believe it would be hard for any special to ever get them away from the Mathews organization.

While I was with Fibre and Fabric my business carried me to Lynn and Lowell, so being a friend of Mathews I dropped into the Item in Lynn and the Sun in Lowell. My story about the Mathews Special Agency led Lynn and Lowell to make contracts with him. In my travels for Printers Ink I always kept an eye out for the interest of the Mathews Agency, and in my travels for the Mathews Agency I kept an eye out for the interests of Printers Ink. This led one special agency to write to Printers Ink claiming that their representative was trying to steal the Providence Journal and Bulletin for the Mathews Agency. Printers Ink wrote a complaining letter and we asked this special to prove his statement, but of course he had no proof. The fact of the matter was that John R. Rathom of Providence, the great publisher of the Bulletin, became very fond of me and did promise that we would represent the Bulletin and Journal; but for the untimely death of this brilliant man Julius Mathews would have represented these two great papers.

We carried for years in Printers Ink a combination page, that is ten or twelve publishers, each paying for a portion of the ad. One day one of the publishers dropped out and I had to find another. I went to see Rathom and sat in front of his office from two to six before he came in. The proposition didn't look good to him and he refused it. Next day I went over to the Hartford Courant office to see Conlon, the publisher. He introduced me to Charles Eddy, who represented his paper. I told Conlon of my proposition and it seemed to look pretty good to him. He asked Eddy if it didn't look good to him. Eddy said no, he would not recommend it. Then he asked me how I made out with Rathom the day before, didn't he refuse it? I didn't want Conlon to know that he had refused it, so I asked Eddy how he knew I had been there. He said he passed me going into the Treasurer's office and knew that I waited a long time for the publisher. I said, "Eddy, you knew me and you passed me without speaking to me? That is wrong. My sister came home from mass and said the priest had given a wonderful sermon on passing people we knew without bowing to them. That each of us had a guardian angel and that it was an insult to the guardian angel to pass a person because we disliked him. I said to my sister Margaret, 'I will wait until some people's heads are turned and I will salute their guardian angels.' " Conlon laughed and said the story was worth the ad. And he stayed in the combination page for many years.

We could have had the Hartford Courant but we represented the weak sister and Mr. Mathews' policy was where we had a publisher in a town not to desert that publisher for a better one. In Lewiston, where he was born and brought up, he represented the Lewiston Sun and refused to represent the great Journal, but in after years he got his reward when the Sun bought the Journal, so now he represents both papers, which have been merged. My special job of course was to get papers for the agency. I went to Fitchburg and saw Mr. Sibley, who sat at the business manager's desk. He said there were five business managers on that paper, himself and four others, the editor, the press man, the stereotyper and the foreman of the composing room. The owner had died leaving his stock to all those men and each man became a business manager. I wanted to talk with them but they were out of town, although they would be on the job at eight o'clock in the morning. I said I would stay over if he would grant me an interview. At eight o'clock I addressed the five of them, told them the story of the Mathews Agency and what I knew we could do for them. I gave each of them a copy of our contract and said, "Gentlemen, hold your meeting, as I leave this town in fifteen minutes." In fifteen minutes they sent for me and signed the contracts. They had a special agency to represent them but our agency was better equipped to gather business for the Sentinel. This contract lasted for more than fifteen years.

The next time I met good old Ben Joy was on the

street. He said, "Say, Dave, how many papers have you got with Mathews?" I told him about thirty-eight. "What are they worth?" I told him about three to four million dollars. "Could you run them as a unit on the Scripp McRae plan?" I told him I could. "All right," he said, "buy them and I will give you the money." I said, "Ben, I don't think I can do it. You asked what they were worth, but that is not what they will sell for. A man's newspaper is as close to him as his wife or daughter. You will have to pay twenty-five per cent more than its worth." He said, "Think it over and the money is waiting." When the World War broke out, Ben Joy resigned his $18,000 job and they trained him at Plattsburg and gave him rank of major. After the war he stayed in Paris, went with Dillon Read, and now he is a partner of J. Pierpont Morgan and looks after their interests in France. Good old Ben Joy, I will never forget your many kindnesses and your faith in me.

CHAPTER XIV

I recommended to Haskell that he hire my friend DeVinney as advertising manager at six thousand dollars a year, which was pretty good money twenty-five years ago. Some time after that the Herald got into difficulty and Mr. Norris came over and took charge of it. DeVinney told me he was going to have a new Special Agency in New York. I said, "No, Captain, you are going to have Beckwith's Special Agency; they are a great agency and Beckwith a fine man." "Just as you say, Dave, I will go to see Beckwith." So Beckwith represented the Herald and I think that connection lasted three or four years. Thus I carried out my promise to Beckwith in New York when he gave me the fifty dollars to come over and look the land over. On his first trip over he said, "I'm going to take you back, you are going to be a member of the Beckwith Special Agency." I said, "No, I am with Mr. Mathews and when I went into his employ he said, 'I know your calibre; some other man who can pay you more money will take you away,' and I said, 'No, Mr. Mathews, I will stay with you at least ten years,' so I am not going with you."

The Captain met two boys on the Herald who were sons of Greene of the famous Nervura. They induced him to leave the Herald and go into the advertising business. When they opened this agency I got the Captain to deposit twenty-five thousand dollars in my friend Ben Joy's bank, which was the Shawmut Bank, and he was then Vice President. In this way I repaid

AN IRISH BOY IN AMERICA 155

Mr. Joy for his kindness in giving me the letters on the Traveler and the letters which I had written for the bank. He in turn looked for some favor to confer on me and he asked me to find out just what the general attitude was towards the Shawmut bank, if there was any hostility to its great size. They were then the leading bank in Boston by a mile, and furthermore he wanted me to find out if I could judge what led men to select a banking institution. I submitted to him a series of interviews much like those I had done for the Boston Traveler which ran into about eighty pages, and he gave me five hundred dollars for doing this job. He said it was a great piece of work.

I have received from Mr. Beckwith since that time fully a hundred favors. I never go to New York without dropping in and enjoying his hospitality. He had a great agency and is a fine character and very lovable. He retired in 1933.

I made many trips to North Adams before I signed up the Transcript. I sold Plummer of the Union. Added to our list were the Post of Hartford, Journal of Meriden, Republican of Waterbury and Telegram and afterwards the Post Telegram of Bridgeport, the Item of Clinton, the Sun of Attleboro, the Day of New London, the Globe of Fall River, afterward the Herald and then again the Globe of Fall River and the Union-Leader of Manchester. I think in all I added about twenty or more papers to the Mathews list. All these papers were sold on long-time contracts. We were to get fifteen per cent of all the foreign business, that is business originating outside of the city of its publication.

One day Mr. Mathews called me into his office and said, "Dave, the little afternoon paper has purchased the Union, the paper which we represented; two men named Knox and Muehling own the Leader. I want you to go up and see them and sell our service at the regular fifteen per cent. I went up to Manchester. I went out to Knox's home to see him, as he was not at his office, and he and his wife and some friends were sitting on the piazza. He took me aside and said, "Well, what can I do for you?" I told him I had been a long time in the newspaper business and had seen many strange things, but this was the first time I saw the tail of a dog turn around and swallow the dog. He laughed very heartily and then I told him the story of the Mathews Agency and what we could do for his two papers. He thought the fifteen per cent arrangement was too much of a tax, but he would let me know in a couple of days.

Two or three days went by and we didn't hear from Knox. Mr. Foster of our office, who has a wise head on his shoulders, said, "Dave, why don't you go up to see Sullivan of 7-20-4 cigars tomorrow morning and then you can see Knox and tell him you are in town to see an advertiser." I went straight from home and took an early train for Manchester and saw Roger Sullivan. He said there was a phone call and telegram for me from the home office. The telegram was to be sure and call the home office. This shows how the Mathews office did things. Nothing was left to chance; in case I got no memo of the telephone call I would get the telegram. The home office said that Knox had written, asking me to come up, as he wanted to have a chat with me. When I was leaving, Roger Sullivan put his hand in a box of cigars and held them out. I took one. He said, "It is a long day—take them all," and I explained to him that the day before I had been in the offices of J. A. Cigar people and they had charged me nine cents for a ten-cent cigar. Sullivan said, "A shut fist never catches anything." They tell me that there never was a young man who went into business in Manchester but Roger Sullivan's name was on his notes in the bank. He had always done a great deal of good in the world and everybody in New England has a kindly story of the founder of the 7-20-4 cigars.

Knox and I talked for an hour or two in the morning and he could not see the fifteen per cent arrangement. He took me to luncheon at his club and asked what I thought about flat rate. I told him I was in favor of a sliding scale of rates for papers of his class. "Why," he said, "my manager, Thomas, who knows advertising forward and backward, is in favor of the flat rate of five cents." I said, "Thomas is wrong. I wrote an article in favor of the flat rate which was published in newspaperdom twenty years ago, as I believed then that a flat rate was the only rate a newspaper should adopt, but in my contact with newspapers I found that the greatest returns would come from a sliding scale." We walked back to the office together. He said that he would never pay fifteen per cent and I stuck out for it like a rock.

As we went into the office, Thomas looked up and said, "Major, the auditor has reported that the average rate of all the business in the Union is six and a quarter cents a line." Knox looked at me and smiled and said, "Lawlor, you win—I will see you in Boston tomorrow and sign those contracts." Up to the minute Thomas spoke, I was defeated. Knox was sure Thomas was right when he fixed on a flat rate of five cents a line for the two papers, and now Thomas showed him the sliding scale gave a greater rate for one paper. This showed Knox we knew our business and would be good people with whom to deal.

When Knox decided to make a contract with Mathews, I said here is a fellow who is going places. He is young, strong, and has the power of decision, a trait I am sorry to say possessed by few New Englanders.

In the West you state your proposition and the man says yes, no, or roll your hoop. Take the case of Ward, who in an hour invested $700,000 in the Federal League Baseball.

Here in Boston you state your proposition and they will think it over, or the board of directors will take it up at their next meeting, or they will have to see father about it. This applies only to the old New Englander. Possibly ducking the arrows of the Indians made them cautious and it remained in the blood. I have sold goods in the middle west and have been pleased with this prompt decision, and I have sold advertising in New England for thirty years and chaffed under the delays in getting decisions.

I went with Knox and a friend one night to some distant town—I think it was Peterboro. Here he made his maiden speech for Theodore Roosevelt. The hall was crowded. Yes, they had the customary oyster stew. He got a great hand, the audience mostly farmers. I thought if this young man gets into politics he will go far.

Going there and back took about three hours, and the talk showed a clear, healthy mind. We who are newspaper men have to learn to appraise men quickly. A half-hour's intimate talk with a man and he will betray his weakness if he has it. Knox is clean-minded, and if he runs for president—and it looks as though he would at the present writing—he will be a very popular candidate.

He came to see me when he was going overseas to

fight. I knew he was with the Rough Riders in 1898, and I thought he might rest on his record. But no, he must do his share and he did, coming back a colonel.

Hearst made him publisher of the Boston American. I said, "You have a tough job, Colonel, the war was easy compared to this." "Don't worry, Dave," he said, "I'll do the job."

Then Hearst made him general manager of all Hearst papers. I believe there are twenty-eight, scattered from Boston to San Francisco. This he kept for four years at a salary said to be $250,000. With a million dollars stored away in safe places, he retired to his papers in Manchester to enjoy the life of a country gentleman. Then Victor Lawson's Chicago Daily News came on the market. The executor wanted cash, but in addition he wanted the owner to be a man of integrity, whose character was above reproach, a man who would be true to the readers of the "News," true to Chicago, a man who would do as well and if possible better than Victor Lawson, the founder. This appealed to Knox and he sought the purchase of the "News" and offered as character witnesses the publishers of daily papers who had papers in the Hearst cities. Every last one of these men said Knox was the man to meet the conditions laid down, and he took over the Daily "News." A recent poll of two thousand newspaper editors showed a preference for Frank Knox as the Republican candidate for president. If a man has the favor of men in his trade, you can label him "a good scout."

Mr. Mathews suggested that I look in on the Waterbury American and try to get them for our list, so one afternoon some twenty-three years ago I arrived in that fine city. There are many fine cities in Connecticut. Hartford might be called the office city, New

Haven the workshops of those great cities. Waterbury is known as the brass city. The L. P. Chase Company make about everything in brass and are known all over the world. They owned the Waterbury American and at one time the Waterbury Republican. The American had a very handsome office; I know the ceiling was lined with gold leaf. I talked with the publisher for a short time and decided he was impossible. I remember saying to myself as I left the office that all the gold in that office is in the ceiling, none in the publisher.

When I went into the Republican office a young fellow came up and gave me a very warm greeting. His name was Copperthorn, advertising manager of the Republican. He said, "I want you to meet Mr. Pape, the publisher," and he told Pape that he had great pleasure in introducing Mr. Lawlor, who made the most wonderful talk on bread that ever was made. Copperthorn was on the Traveler when we opened the bakery in Boston, and he was one of the men to whom I gave the printed story of the making of a loaf of bread. This glowing introduction of Copperthorn's was a fine introduction to Pape and we chatted for about an hour on Printers Ink and the Julius Mathews Agency. I made no effort to sell him. I invited him over to dinner at the Elton, but he said that he had been out for two nights and his wife would never stand his being out that night. I said, "I think if you tell her you are with a good fellow she will be delighted to let you off." He said he would go to dinner if I would go to the theatre with him afterward.

We finished dinner about quarter of seven, which was an hour too early to go to the show, so I purchased a handful of cigars and invited him up to my room. I asked if I might lie down for that hour as I was not feeling very well. This was the truth, as I was sore and in pain when on my feet. We got talking about the Republican, his ideals, and the problems that were confronting him. Then he told me of his struggles in Waterbury and I told him of my experience in Fall River, New York and Chicago, and how we had met in our organization similar problems to his and how they were met and what the results were. We smoked and chatted for quite a while, but in all my talks I would from time to time introduce the agency into the talk much as a weaver would weave a pattern in the cloth. My object naturally was to create a desire for him to engage our services. I saw that he was all right, that he had the stuff that made a great publisher and it was only a matter of time before he would have the great paper in Waterbury. I succeeded in this because two or three times during the talk he asked if I would not invite him to join our organization. I finally suggested that he come up with me in the morning and have a talk with Mr. Mathews and I would recommend Mr. Mathews to take his paper.

Pape rose from his chair, clapped his hands and said, "That is settled, now let's go to the show." He pulled out his watch and said, "By George, it is ten past eleven." We had talked from quarter of seven until ten past eleven, neither of us having any idea of the flight of time. I got to know Mr. Pape very intimately as the years went on, and he now owns not only the Republican daily and Sunday, but also the American. He has a very fine mechanical plant and he prints the colored sections for not only his own city but Bridgeport, Springfield, Toronto and Montreal. He had three boys and at the same time one of them was in Annapolis and another in West Point. They graduated the same year. The boy who was in the navy is now assistant publisher.

I have kept my friendship with him and his good wife all through the years and I value it very highly.

Pape and his good wife were in the office one day about fifteen years ago, and insisted that I join the luncheon which Mr. Mathews was giving them. Pape began to tell about the great clock industry in Waterbury and I told the party about the time Mary and I were contemplating getting married. We had very little money and what we had had to go a long way, so I said we would not buy a clock nor a lamp. I had, as reporter, attended one hundred weddings and there was always a surplus of clocks and lamps, so somebody would give us one or two of each, so that was provided for. Strange to relate, when we looked over the presents, no one gave a clock or a lamp to us. The first working day after our honeymoon I found a man who was contemplating advertising a gorgeous lamp. It sure was a beauty and I made an advertising contract with him. I explained that all advertisers were entitled to a reading notice with every contract, and this could be furnished by the advertiser, but I would be glad to write it if he would give me a lamp. He said that if he liked the notice he would give me what I desired. In an hour I was back with the most wonderful story of a lamp that ever was written. I wanted that lamp and in my story Aladdin's lamp would have had to take second place. Had it ever been printed it would have been a classic, because I wanted that lamp so badly that I wrote a thousand words about it. The prospective advertiser asked when it would be published. I said at the first appearance of the advertisement. He gave me the lamp but for some reason the agreement to advertise was never carried out and he never got his notice. We got a twenty-five cent alarm clock to tide us over until we were in a position to buy a clock and when that clock wore out we bought another alarm clock and now after twenty-five years we owned a house, some pretty things, but still had an alarm clock.

Mr. Mathews laughed, Mrs. Pape smiled and Pape roared. About ten days afterward, we were having our silver anniversary, and a host of friends came to our little house. I don't know how they all got in. We probably pushed the walls out and the roof up. Mr. Mathews sent a clock by his good wife who has since passed away, leaving him a lonely man, and a beautiful clock came from Waterbury, the gift of the Papes, and one of the lights of the Church, a Right Reverend Monseigneur, came with a clock under his arm. Some years ago when I began to realize the real true things of this world, I adopted a practice of saying a little prayer whenever I hear the clock strike, so these three good men, I feel, have been amply repaid for their gifts.

One day a nice young fellow came into my office and said, "You are always doing a good turn for somebody, so I came in to do you a good turn. Put on your coat and come with me." He brought me to see the Madonna Gonzaga which was in a private studio. Several people were on their knees saying their prayers and we joined them. Christmas Eve I brought Mary in to see it, and we purchased a copy of it painted by Miss Hammond. The copy is exquisite. Father Glot told me that the original is the most beautiful painting in the world. He was in the Louvre at Paris for fourteen years before he entered the priesthood so he should know paintings.

When we came out of the studio I met my young

friend and said, "Well, John Prior, I have purchased a copy of the Madonna and am taking it home with me."

"Good," said John, "you will never see a poor day again." I invited John to come with me as I wanted to buy a prayer book for my secretary. I bought two and handed one to John and said, "Here, you will find that which will do you more good than anything else in the world."

Mary wanted to go into Bacon's Department Store next, and we stood near the door while she went upstairs. Fred Kerry, the general manager of the store, was talking with two of his partners and he turned around and saw me. He came over and said, "Dave, I would like to make the same arrangement with you that you had with George Dutton." My friend nudged me and whispered in my ear, "The Madonna is working for you." I did a lot of business with Fred Kerry. In addition to the original agreement which he faithfully kept, I wrote all the introductions for his advertising when the firm got into difficulties. Kerry and I were having lunch one day with two bank men who were in charge of their affairs. One of them turned to me and said, "We were telling Fred this morning that were you the advertising manager since they started in business, we would not be here now."

The Madonna hangs over my mantle. One stormy night an old priest came in to see us and without a word he knelt in front of the picture for nearly half an hour. What passed between the Blessed Mother and himself I do not know, but when he got off his knees his face had a beautiful smile.

Theodore Boudenwein of New London was Secretary of State. He had a dandy paper in New London, and I assume that he still has this fine newspaper. I walked into his office one day and told him I represented the Julius Mathews Special Agency. He backed away from the office railing and help up his hand and said, "I have had Katz" (another special agency). As he retreated to his office I shouted to him, "And the cat had kittens." He came back to the railing and said, "Just what do you mean, sir?" I said, "You invite me into your office and I'll tell you about it." When I finished my story he agreed to sign my contract and would mail it to me the next day.

When we received the contract in Boston the next day, it was signed but he had written in ink below the signature a reservation which nullified the contract. I called him on the phone and said I received his contract and was coming down on the ten o'clock train and would meet him in New London at twelve-thirty. He agreed to meet me, but was not there at twelve-thirty, nor one, nor two, nor three. No one had any trace of him. I walked up and down in front of his office from twelve-thirty to five-thirty and he slipped in the back door. I walked to the railing and he met me and said, "I suppose you are going to give me hell." I said, "I have never given anyone hell in my life." We walked back to his office and I stood over him. I laid the contract before him. I said, "You take a pen and you cross out that which you have written; it nullified the contract." "I won't do it!" I clenched my hand and shouted, "You won't," and he said, "No, I won't do it." And he reached over and got a pair of scissors and cut from the contract that part which he had written as a reservation. He said, "Will that do?" I said, "Fine," and could have kissed him.

I often dropped into the office of the Bridgeport Telegram. It was owned by a man named Hills. I didn't make much progress with him, but I continued dropping in until one day Mr. Marsh, the business manager, told me that I didn't need to come any more, that the paper had been sold. I asked who had bought it and he said a man named McNeil, a coal operator in New York. I asked where he lived or where I could see him and finally got the reluctant admission that they had an office on a nearby street. I talked with Kenneth McNeil, who told me his father had bought it, but his brother Archie was to be publisher, and he was in New York for a day or two, but would be back. I sketched to Kenneth what sort of agency we were and what we could do for his brother and he suggested I write him and ask for an appointment.

I said to Kenneth, "Do you think your brother will get the letter if I write it?" He said, "Sure, he'll get it; Uncle Sam is on the job and you have the correct address, there is no reason why he won't get it, is there?"

I said, "I don't know, but sometimes letters go astray." I went to our New York office and wrote a letter to Archie McNeil, saying I would be in New York for four or five days, and if he would write me in care of New York office I could see him on the way back. I didn't hear from him and I waited for about ten days and had an inspiration to make a special trip to Bridgeport. I found Mr. McNeil in his office with his editor. I told him who I was and that I had written him a perfectly good letter and had had no answer and that he looked like a gentleman who answered his mail and I could not understand it. He and the editor exchanged glances and he said, "Why, Mr. Lawlor, I received no letter from you." "Well," I said, "I asked your brother if you would get it if I wrote you and he told me you would." We talked about the representation of his newspaper and he said, "Well, now here, this is Tuesday; you come down Thursday and father will be here and you make the talk to the whole of us Thursday." On that day I was in the office, introduced to the father. The editor was there and they called for Mr. Marsh. I made the talk about the agency, exhibit A—B—C, a fairly good talk, and then sat back to answer any questions that they might ask. I could see the talk had made a good impression upon Archie, his father and the editor, but Mr. Marsh looked like the sphinx.

The elder McNeil said, "How does this thing look to you?"

Marsh asked, "Do I understand, Mr. Lawlor, that we are to tie up to your agency for a period of years and pay you fifteen per cent on all business for that period if you don't increase our business?" I could see through the corner of my eye old man McNeil stiffen. I said, "I can answer that question with a story, Mr. Marsh." Everybody leaned back, because a story is usually received as a fellow receives a kiss from a girl. I said, "Father Power preached on Miracles and after the mass was over Casey went into the vestry and as the priest was disrobing, said, 'Father, that was a great sermon but I don't quite see what a miracle is.' The good father answered, 'Any event in the natural world but out of its established order and possibly only by the intervention and execution of divine power. There were miracles in Our Lord's time and from time to time miracles happen today, at Lourdes, Ste. Anne's and many other places. Whenever and wherever the Good Lord wants a miracle to take place, it takes place,' and the priest started to leave the vestry for his house by the roadside, but Casey was not satisfied and plucked his sleeve and said, 'I wish you would bring it home to me just what a miracle is.' Now

Father Power was a saintly man, but he had a touch of Irish temper. 'Walk ahead of me, Mr. Casey, until I think of a definition of a miracle that you would understand.' As he passed by the reverend father, the saintly man lifted his foot and gave Casey a powerful kick that landed him in the roadside. Casey rose with tears in his eyes and cried, 'Father, why did you kick me?'

" 'Did you feel it?' said the Father. 'Sure I felt it,' said Casey. 'Well,' said the good priest, 'if you didn't that would have been a miracle.' "

Everyone roared. "Marsh," I said, "if we don't increase your business, it will be a miracle." Marsh looked at me and never even smiled, but got out of his chair and left the office. McNeil signed the contract and said, "That was a great story."

Some years later when they bought the Post there were a host of agencies after the two papers. They had stories about Mathews' weakness in New York and Mathews' weakness somewhere else, all of which were told to me by McNeil. I had been reading Emerson's book on efficiency, so I showed how the agency was organized and while the headquarters were in Boston yet troops were easily mobilized and our men could cover by means of the railroad any place where there was an agency or an advertiser. Archie said, "I guess you are right, Dave," and he signed the contract for the Mathews Agency to represent the Post Telegram. We looked after their business for many years until Flicker and his friends bought the property and they had other men. Mathews gave them great service and it was a pity that Flocker could not see the light.

In the city of Salem, Robin Damon owned the News. He was known among newspaper editors as the great economist. He had written and lectured on how publishers could save money by making their margins smaller and reducing the white space wherever possible. One day I dropped into his fair city and offered him $275,000 for the News. He offered to sell it to me for $300,000. I had explained to him who had sent me and he knew that the United Shoe Machinery Company were backers of the whole affair. Then I took up with him the matter of special representation of the News and he could not see it. Too much money for what he would get out of it. He said, "Let me ask you a question. Suppose an agency offers you $450 for an advertisement and your rate card figures $500, what would you do?" "Why," I said, "endeavor to get him to come up to the $500." "Well, suppose he would not pay it?" And I answered, "We would let him stay out until hell froze over. There is only one way to do honest business, and that is to treat everybody alike." "Well," he said, "the way I do it, I take the $450 and put it in my pants' pocket, but if I had you to represent me I would be $450 out! What do you think of that?" I said, "The Good Book says, Mr. Damon, that your sins will find you out." He got very serious for a minute and said, "I guess that is right. Bring up your contract and let me have a look at it."

The next day I brought in the contracts all filled out. We had a very formidable looking contract which covered about two pages, telling about the party of the first part and the party of the second part. Nothing was left to good faith. Damon sat down and read it over, rose from the chair and said, "I will never sign that contract." He walked away from me and I took off my coat, put it on a peg, pulled the chair over beside his desk and lit a cigar. He walked up and down and up and down the office and came back and sat down and read the contract over again. He pounded the desk and said, "Never! Never will I sign such a contract—it is damnable." I took out another cigar, lit it, smoked away for ten minutes. He, walking up and down the office. He sat down at the desk again, read over the contract, dipped his pen in the ink and signed them both and handed them to me. I thanked him and said, "That is the best job you ever did; now there is one more matter and that is the matter of Boston Store advertising." I told him he was five miles further out than Lynn and five miles made some difference and we would get the business for him at thirty-five per cent commission. Years later he doubted this and Mr. Mathews brought out his contract and he said, "Mr. Mathews, Dave had me hypnotized that day." I brought a lot of retail advertising in the Lynn and Salem papers and was getting a very good thing out of it when the merchants in both cities prevailed on the publishers to refuse business from Boston. They did so and I lost the commissions on a lot of hard work that I had done."

After the great Salem fire I again saw Damon about the sale of his paper. This time he asked $350,000. "Why," I said, "you only asked $300,000 before and now when your city is in ruins you ask $350,000." He smiled and said, "The city will build up again. Since I gave you the final price I have Mathews working for me and the paper is worth the price I ask." Then he told me he was making more than $50,000 a year. I liked Damon and I was sorry when I heard that he and his chauffeur tried to cut a corner and were killed.

I must have made about ten trips to Haverhill to try to sell our service to Moran, the business manager.

He was what the boys on the road called a tough egg. That the reader may not get a wrong impression, he was a really fine gentleman, but he was hard to sell. One day he sold himself, and it came about this way. He said to me, "Did you know that every man that ever went into the shoe business failed?" I leaned back in my chair and laughed and said, "What about Douglas, Little, Plant," and I named four or five of the manufacturers. He said, "Listen, just a few drops in the bucket." Then he produced a list about a yard long. I said, "That is surprising, how do you account for it?" "They went into business, studied conditions and made good. Conditions changed and they did not change to meet new conditions. Younger men came in and saw how things were changing and they met them and the old fellows fell by the wayside. You know we are placed on this old world, all of us, and it is a great ball turning towards us and if we do not dig with out hands and our feet to hold our place it rolls us under." I said, "I guess that is true. I was reading a page in the Boston Herald printed in 1863. A banquet was given General McClellan by the four hundred leading merchants in Boston. I went over the list of the four hundred and found there were just three names whose signs were still over the door. They thought that they knew all about the business and they didn't dig and were turned under."

"You know, Moran," I continued, "Professor James says the average man is an old fogey at twenty-four. You are one-half a fogey—you realize those changing conditions, but you don't act. The Special Agency business has grown up and there is a new and better way of covering advertising than can be done by the local representatives." Moran scratched his head and said, "You can give me your contract."

I never had much to do with politics in my early days, nothing at all except vote. About twenty-three years ago Fahey, the publisher of the Traveler, sent for me and said, "Did you know that James J. Storrow was running for mayor?" I said, "No, tell me about it." "Well," he said, "Storrow is a very rich banker, a good man, and he wants to be mayor of Boston. He has an advisory board of fifteen men, five magazine men, five publishers and five advertising agents. They want someone to crystallize their thoughts and act as press agent for Mr. Storrow. At the last meeting that matter was taken up and strange to relate, you are the only man who was mentioned by the fifteen." I had been writing to the magazine men and the newspaper men about Printers Ink and had been writing to the advertising men about the advertising in Lynn and Salem. These letters attracted a lot of attention, so naturally I came to their minds. Fahey continued that he had talked the matter over with Mr. Storrow, who had asked was I a high-brow and being assured that I was not, he wanted to know me. I asked Mr. Storrow for two hundred and fifty dollars a week for the six weeks of the campaign. He said it was too much, but he would give me two hundred dollars and I accepted this. It was a part-time arrangement of course, and I would devote my attention to Mr. Mathews' interests and my work would be done mostly in Mr. Mathews' office, though he provided an office and secretary for me in the Kimball building.

Everything went along smoothly. Mr. Storrow gave an order to the Hotel Bellevue that all we ate, drank or smoked be charged to his account. The only thing that he specified was that when cigars were called for the price should be three for a dollar.

The first day he said to me, "I have a letter from the labor unions asking me to pledge myself to only employ union labor in every department. What shall I say to them?"

"Tell them you are going to be mayor of Boston as a whole, both union and non-union," I replied.

"That's good sense and good business," he said with a smile. I liked Storrow. Naturally I got to know him very intimately. I was at his house, and it is a beautiful home in Lincoln. I believe that he ran for mayor of the city of Boston for the same reason that led the Minute Men to grab a rifle and hurry to Bunker Hill. Some ten days before the election some of the advisory committee suggested that we run on the front page of each paper every day from that time up to election a hundred or two hundred-line advertisement, each advertisement being an indictment of John F. Fitzgerald, who was running against Mr. Storrow. I opposed this. I said, "If you do this thing, you will unite the people of Irish blood and Catholic faith and they will go against Storrow. You will make a martyr out of Fitzgerald and there are a lot of fair-minded people who will get the impression he is abused and they will vote for him."

I was overruled and every day John F. Fitzgerald was charged with doing some dishonest act. Mr. Storrow got on the job every night speaking. He addressed rallies and gatherings up to twelve each night and then would talk with his committee until two. No man can stand that strain and be normally minded. Had he been in his right mind he would never have consented to what was done against Fitzgerald. The night before the election I saw the crowd pouring into the Fitzgerald rally at Tremont Temple, and I studied them on the way in. The set expression on their faces showed their determination, and I said that night to Mary that Storrow would not be elected. Storrow missed by 1,750 votes, and the most surprised man in Boston was John F. Fitzgerald. Up to the week before the election he was beaten to a frazzle. A day or two afterward I went in to see Mr. Storrow, and he wrote out a check for $1200 and thanked me for what I had done and said, "Mr. Lawlor, if I had followed your advice I would have been elected mayor of Boston." Storrow was a great friend of the newsboys and the Boy Scouts, and he and his good wife did a lot of kindly things while he was here.

Some eight years ago I dropped in to see James M. Curley, now Governor of Massachusetts, who was running for mayor of Boston against John R. Murphy. "Jim," I said, "I want to give you some advice. Take that article of John Bantry's of the Post, put it into booklet form and sent it to every voter in Boston. I don't know whether he meant to be friendly or not, but it has in it a message which will elect you. I will take excerpts from it and have our friend Donnelly put it into poster space. In addition to that I would suggest that you reconcile your enemies and you have quite a few of them. You will get nowhere fighting them, you will only make the fight more bitter." He smiled and said, "Dave, I guess you are right." A month after he was elected I met him coming down Beacon Street in Boston with his wife. He put out one hand to stop me and said to his wife, "I want you to meet my friend, Dave Lawlor—it was his advice that made me mayor of Boston again."

James Michael Curley is a great man, bitterly hated by his enemies, warmly loved by his friends. He made a good mayor and is making a greater governor. He does not follow precedents—he makes them. Quick of mind, very eloquent, courageous, he does what he believes best and sticks to it. He was the first of the leaders here to pick Roosevelt for President. The party was against this and for Smith, but he stuck to the finish. Then he won the State for governor by a tremendous majority. He makes mistakes, but so does everyone. It is like playing a piano—great artists strike a false note at rare intervals, but those who never play never make a mistake.

I like Jim Curley. He has always been nice to me, even though he would not do some of the things I believe it would have been well for him to do. Maybe this is one of the signs of his greatness. It was he who caused the annuity system to be applied to all the employees of the City of Boston. Now when they reach the retirement age they may live in comfort for the rest of their lives. Roosevelt's Social Security Act will in time perform a similar service for such as you and me.

One day on my rounds for Printers Ink I found my friend Frank S. Baker of Cleveland, who was publisher of the Boston Traveler. He surely was delighted to see me. He told me the Traveler was purchased by his father, Bert Holden of Cleveland and Mr. Winslow of the United Shoe Machinery Corporation, and they had sent him on to be publisher of the Traveler. As I was leaving after my call, he said, "Here, Dave, just a minute." He opened a drawer in his desk and held out a handful of letters. "I wish you would look these letters over and give me your opinion of them." I recognized them as the letters I had written for Ben Joy. I told him that I wrote them and he said he knew Fahey did not have the advertising knowledge to write them although they bore his signature. I used to go in often to see Frank, and we became very intimate. James C. Higgins, the publisher of a little paper up in Newburyport, came into our office one day and told our Mr. Foster that he was in trouble. He said he had occasion to do a little favor for Mr. Winslow of the United Shoe Machinery and they had become very friendly. Winslow wanted to do something for him and his money bought the Gloucester Times; Winslow wanted him to go in and see what the deuce was the matter with the Traveler, as they were losing $180,000 a year. Higgins said he knew nothing whatever about metropolitan newspapers, and how could he go into a big paper and make an intelligent report on what should be done. Foster said, "Let's go in and see Dave—he knows about newspapers."

We talked the matter over and the plan which was carried out was suggested by Mr. Foster. He said, "Why don't you have Dave interview twenty-five men, five publishers who own newspapers, five advertising managers of stores and five advertising managers of agencies and five heads of agencies and five men who represent the rank and file."

Higgins thought this was good and the job was assigned to me, so I reported the interviews. No man knew that he was being interviewed. I would drop in, turn the talk on the Globe and Herald, and during the talk bring up the Traveler and ask what the matter was with it and what they'd do with it if they owned it and had a million dollars. Then while the matter was fresh in my mind I would go back to the office and dictate the story, wipe it from my mind and go after another interview. Higgins told me Winslow was delighted with the fine job he did and he made him business manager of the Traveler, Mr. Baker still retaining the title of publisher. I told

Frank Baker about those interviews, what was said and what was done, that McGregor of Houghton & Dutton said the damn paper didn't stand for anything and didn't fit anywhere, and he was right. Frank Baker was a good newspaper man and of course today he is a far better one since he has had nearly twenty more years' experience. He said, "I'll tell you what we will do. You answer McGregor, put on a campaign for the Traveler, and I will give you a hundred dollars a week and a three-year contract." Higgins assented to this proposition. Contract was made at the Julius Mathews Agency, but Baker said, "No, my contract is with David Lawlor."

The plan was that I was to go to luncheon with Frank Baker every day and he was to tell me what his troubles were, based on the reports of the advertising solicitors. He said to me one day, "Now there is R. H. White; I have been here two years and have never been able to see him. How can I get anywhere with him?" So I wrote a note to R. H. White. The opening lines were, "This is a letter to one who had made history from one who has history to make," and I brought out the fact that I had been for two years there as publisher of the Traveler, and he always refused to see me, and that as he never did any advertising in the Traveler, wasn't it a fair inference that the Traveler readers were just as dead to his store as if they were tucked away in the old Granary burying ground?

This letter, of course, bore Baker's signature. The next day the advertising manager sent for him and gave him one half-page advertisement, then one half-page again and then a whole page, and at the end of two weeks Mr. Baker got a personal letter from Mr. White, a very nice and friendly letter, apologizing for not having seen him in the two years, and that on receipt of the letter he told his advertising man to give it a try out and he was glad to report that the results had been very satisfactory and hereafter the Traveler would carry his business.

I wrote a letter to McGregor on what the Traveler stood for and this was followed by where the Traveler fits. These letters were also sent to Mr. Butler, who owned the Gilchrist and Butler Stores and I think one other store. In each of the letters the final paragraph was that while the letters were personal to them, that if they had no objections they would be printed on the editorial page of the Traveler. As I remember them, they probably contained a thousand words and they looked pretty good to Mr. Baker and me, so they were set in pica and appeared on the editorial page over Frank's signature. Frank said that he had a lot of favorable comment on these editorials and he was sorry that he could not say that I wrote them.

Part of the campaign was to send every day to every man who advertised in any paper a postal card telling him about the Traveler. If the advertiser was in the Globe Monday he got his card the next day. We had a pretty big list of outs but every day some work was done. The campaign was modelled much after the one I had put on in Pittsburgh.

A few days after these editorials were printed Frank and I went to luncheon at the Georgian because President Taft was to be there. Butler was at the door, he saw Frank and his face lighted up and he said, "Come in to see me this afternoon." This tickled Frank, for he was not getting a line of Butler's advertising. Frank came into my office late in the afternoon and said, "What do you think? I had a wonderful interview with Butler. He produced both editorials. The first one was what the Traveler stands for. He said, 'Baker, you are not producing that kind of paper.' I said, 'I know, but that is my ideal; you are not producing the store service you want.' Butler said, 'If I thought Winslow would let you make that kind of paper I will make a $50,000 contract in advertising every year for three years and meet every raise that is warranted in circulation.'" I told Baker he ought to see Winslow. Then Mr. Winslow sent for me.

It seems that Frank had recommended me to come as advertising manager at a salary of $10,000 a year. It was a Saturday afternoon I was to meet Mr. Winslow at one o'clock. We talked until six. A very kindly old man. He said, "What do you think prompted this offer of Butler's?" "Well," I said, "I don't know, but I believe what is in his mind is this: He likes Baker and he likes the thought of a paper such as outlined in that editorial. He wants to give the American a kick in the pants for something they have done to him, because he told Frank he was going to quit the American if he went into the Traveler. Back of all this I feel Mr. Butler has in mind that he had bitten off a little more than he can chew. He has three stores. He can sail along fine in smooth waters, but he wants to be in a position if the storm arises that he can come to you and say, 'Here is a statement of my business; you own the First National Bank, will you arrange for me to borrow one hundred or two hundred thousand dollars for my business?'" Winslow said, "I guess you have hit it all right. Now what would you do if I gave you a million to make the Traveler; tell me how you would build the paper." So when I told him my story he said, "Well, I have made the Herald a proposition; if they do not come in on my terms, Mr. Lawlor, I will make you manager and I will give you the million to make the Traveler." I knew about this negotiation for this amalgamation because Higgins had told me all about it. The Herald took over the Traveler and three men were appointed to direct the affairs. Each was to get $15,000 apiece. The three men were Farley, Higgins and O'Brien. They stopped paying me my $100 per week when they united and Mathews cut my drawing account from $75 per week to $40. So I went down to see Mr. Farley and asked how about it. He waved his hand and said, "That is all off; the contract is no good, dead. I am sorry, but cannot do anything about it." "Why, Mr. Farley," I said, "while you probably know more law than I do, yet I reported law courts for five years and I assure you that contract is good." He dismissed me with the tone of "Run along, little boy, I don't play marbles with you." Three or four days later I again took up this matter and he assured me that there was nothing doing nor would there be anything. The next day I came in again and he seemed just a little put out with this persistence of mine. I said, "Mr. Farley, here is a note from Brandeis, Nutter and Dunbar and in this note it says my contract is legally good." Farley read it, passed it over to Higgins, put his finger in his vest and said, "I can get them to write a counter one for $250." I had paid $50 for mine. I said, "That may be true, but they will go into court with my case. Will I ask them to bring proceedings in the morning?" He said, "Wait, don't be in such a hurry; give us a chance to think." A day or two afterward Mr. Higgins came in to see Mr. Mathews and he had a certified check for $4500. He said, "This is the best settlement we can make, and I would advise you to take it." We accepted it and I went home that night with $2250 in my pants' pocket. I never had so much money in my life.

Farley didn't stay very long in the Herald, and Higgins became General Manager. He offered me $10,000 a year if our agency would represent the Herald in the foreign field. He would not pay $15,000 which we tried to get. He told me Mr. Winslow gave him his personal check for $10,000 for putting the deal over between the Herald and the Herald Traveler. I liked Jim Higgins and he liked me. It was I who urged him to put on the rotogravure pages which bring the Herald so much business.

He made a great newspaper out of the Herald Traveler. He had as his assistant E. W. Preston, now the general manager of both papers. Preston came to this city some twenty years ago. He was without friends, but he was a man of great energy and ability. He had an idea of starting a suburban advertising service, that is for the merchants of Boston to advertise in the daily papers within fifty miles of Boston, one piece of copy to be furnished and they would make mats for the newspapers. They found that we had Lynn and Salem tied up, and they came to see us and we made arrangements so that they could sell those two papers with their own list.

This brought Preston to the notice of Higgins, who owned the newspaper in Lynn, Gloucester and Newburyport. After a little while Higgins asked me to give up the Lynn Item and take on his paper in Lynn. This Mr. Mathews would not do, so he gave the representation of the Lynn News, Gloucester Times and Newburyport News to Preston. In a little while he brought Preston into the Herald as advertising manager. The new advertising manager had visions, worked hard and saw that everybody else worked. He went after every business in the city, not only in display and classified. He knew it was hard to get business without men and he had solicitors to cover each line of activity. At one time he had ninety-six advertising solicitors.

I laughed at Preston when he told me that he was going to carry more lineage than the Globe and Post, but he made good his boast, leading them all with more than sixteen million lines of advertising. He had of course the help of two good newspapers, the Herald and the Traveler. The Herald made very little gain in circulation, but the Traveler leaped from 80,000 to 180,000 a day. He had the good sense to give the advertisers moderate rates, both papers for twenty-eight cents a line, local. Higgins in the meantime began to wobble in his mind. He was very fond of his wife and when she passed away he never recovered from the shock. He is now in an asylum. The union of the Herald-Traveler was joining two daily newspapers which were each losing $200,000 a year. The Herald gave the Traveler prestige and the Traveler gave the Herald quantity of circulation. The two factors brought business when properly sought after by able men.

Some time after the merging of the Herald-Traveler, Butler found himself in financial difficulties and instead of going to Winslow, whom I believe would have helped him, he took another way out of his difficulties and was found dead in his office one morning.

I met Robert Lincoln O'Brien, the editor of the Herald-Traveler, shortly after he went to the Herald. One of my co-workers in Mr. Mathews's office came in to see me one day and said he was a resident of Walpole and he had asked Robert Lincoln O'Brien to lecture there the following Sunday night. O'Brien promised he would do it on condition that I go with him. I told Everett that it could not be me that Mr. O'Brien wished to accompany him—it must be Mr. Mathews, surely a great man like O'Brien would not expect a humble solicitor to be his guest on that occasion. Mr. Everett went down to see O'Brien and said he was getting old and his hearing was evidently playing him false, that he understood it was Mr. Lawlor, but of course it was Mr. Mathews, O'Brien said no, it was Dave Lawlor, and if he didn't go that there would be no talk. I refused to go. I told him my leisure moments were few and far between and that I didn't feel I could spend them in Walpole when I could have a far better time at home. Mr. Mathews urged me to go and find out what it was all about. I finally consented to go and we went down on the train to Walpole the next day, and he surely was delightful company. He told me of his early life and he gave a fine address on taxation. When we came back he told me he had had the most enjoyable day of his life.

O'Brien stayed on the Herald for fifteen years, disagreed with Preston, and one day the Herald had a nice editorial telling how sorry they were that he had resigned, and wished him luck wherever he would go.

Robert Lincoln O'Brien is a wonderful man. He is just my age. He did a great job for the Transcript and a greater one for the Herald. He sees newspapers from the editorial angle, but unfortunately the advertising angle is five times as important.

President Hoover was looking for an Eastern man to head the tariff commission and the biggest man he could see was O'Brien so he sent for him and offered him the chairmanship. O'Brien was not recommended for the place by anyone, he did not ask for it, expect it, or desire it, but he is chairman of the Tariff Commission.

Some enemy sowed cockle in the wheatfield of the Ward Baking Company. One day all the newspapers came out with a front page story that the board of health had found plaster of paris in Ward's bread. This was about twenty-one years ago, after Wards had been making bread for nine years and had built up a wonderful business due to the excellence of their product. The president of the Ward Baking Company came into my office and said, "Dave, we are in a peck of trouble. I want you to write an ad for all the Boston papers and offer to reward $500 to anyone who can find anything harmful in Ward's Tip Top Bread." I said, "What is the story?" Then he told me that some months before they had brought their problem to the Mellon Institute in Pittsburgh. They told the head of this great institute that a formula was prepared in the Pittsburgh office for all their plants, but the results differed in every plant and they could not understand it. Mellon's people said if they would give $10,000 to the institute for research work they would make a report. It developed at the Institute when considering Ward's problem they had the same flour, same yeast, same milk and when they came to water they put a question mark. They made an analysis of the different waters used in the various plants and found they differed greatly. The thought came to the men in charge of the Ward problem that if they could standardize the water the product would be the same. They knew that the finest beer in the world was brewed in England. They got samples of that water, put the yeast into it and found that one-half the amount of yeast could do the work that more than double could do in hard water.

Calcium Sulphate and Ammonium chloride was made as a preparation and added to the waters at the plants and the results were very good, the bread in all plants was the same and Ward discovered that he was only using one-half of the yeast, so he made known his discovery after getting a process patent from the United States Government, and the bakers of the country outside of his zone of activity bought this new preparation, which was shipped in bags to the various plants. The health officer of the City of Boston, acting on advices received from some one, confiscated this preparation which was going to the Ward plant in Cambridge and gave out a story to the newspapers that plaster of paris was being used in Ward's bread. I went to the various editors and told them the true story, also informed them they were guilty of criminal libel, that Ward was a fighter, had the money and would not take a licking. All the papers immediately refused to publish any more about plaster of paris and the Post said editorially that Ward was right. Ward told me to handle all the Boston advertising and select any agency I wished, so I gave the business to my friend, Charles O'Malley, whom I had met in Pittsburgh, a friendship continued until this day.

Then a bill was introduced in the legislature regarding the label on bread. If the ingredients were only composed of flour, yeast, salt, milk and water, it didn't have to be mentioned on the label, which would be about one-half inch, but if it contained any other ingredient, there should be a four-inch label telling everything that went into the bread. We had a hearing before the committee and the brilliant John A. Sullivan represented the city of Boston and Dr. Jordan, the milk inspector, was there with various samples of this preparation. When the company's turn came, they had brought a dozen witnesses that were men very high in their professions, and they told how this product really improved the bread. Their testimony covered about two pages but only got a small amount of space in the newspapers. Labor Unions were all there in favor of the bill; Ward was a non-union bakery, as were all the other bakeries. I remember the president of the plaster union making a very impassioned speech. His conclusion was, "We are told that this generation lacks the stamina of our fathers and forefathers but Ward is going to fix all that by introducing plaster of paris in the bread we eat so that we will have everything in our systems our ancestors had."

The committee reported favorably on the bill. I called the headquarters in New York and suggested that we appeal to the public. I said, "Let's take a two-page ad in all the papers here Sunday and give the testimony of all these great authorities on food and health." They said, "Go to it," and the next Sunday a double truck appeared in all the newspapers and during the week the Legislature met. The company won their fight. The loss of business to the bakery on account of this was more than half a million dollars. There was one incident in connection with this that often makes me laugh.

Some Englishman wisely said that outside the line of activity of any specialist he is a silly ass. The amount of "Arcady" in a loaf of bread would easily fit on the head of a pin. Yet a health officer of the City of Boston had at this hearing what was supposed to be loaves of bread made out of the plaster of paris. There was no flour, no yeast or anything that enters into bread, so what he showed was nothing but loaves of plaster of paris. He told the story of baking those and he wanted to show the members of the committee what would happen when this compound was used, so he laid down a half dozen bricks which he had baked out of this product.

I had some correspondence with Mr. R. B. Ward shortly afterward about an undertaking I had in mind and he advised me not to go into it, but if I did he would be glad to keep his promise to me and send me the money that was necessary. I went over to New York to see him and he greeted me very affectionately and told me he was not feeling very well, as he had a pain in his shoulder. I said to put a plaster on it and it would be all right. He said, "Dave, it is worrying me; I'm really afraid." I said, "Go out into the sun, see the flowers, hear the birds," and he smiled and shook hands with me, but I could see that he was in no mood to discuss what was in our minds. A day or two afterward he died.

William Ward was invited back to the Ward Baking Company as president. I met Will Ward when he opened the bakery in Boston. He was just out of college then and his father sent him over to learn the business. He used to come up to my home and we enjoyed his company. I never appreciated the fact that this boy had it in him to be the great business man that he turned out to be. A little while ago he gave to the City of New York a thousand acres of land to be used for the poor men and women of New York, and he gave a million dollars endowment to carry it on. A few years ago while in apparently wonderful health, he went into his office, folded his arms and without a struggle went to join his father. His estate showed that he left $15,000,000 which he made from the time he left college. He was only forty-two years old and had he lived I believe he would have done great things.

CHAPTER XV

The Boston American sent a letter to our office one day asking me to call on Mr. Bogart, temporary publisher. Mr. Bogart said that two of the big merchants of Boston had called on Mr. Carvalho and recommended me for the position of publisher of the Boston American. He had orders to look me up and make a report. The job didn't look extraordinarily good to me for I had seen publishers come and go, quite a few of them. I explained to him that I had been with Hearst in Chicago and New York and was let out of their service as they didn't think I was hardly the average. Mr. Bogart was appointed publisher and I have seen quite a few new publishers, I don't know just how many, at least seven or eight since that time, some twelve or fifteen years ago. They have had a lot of fine able men on the Boston American in the last twenty-five years, but none of them could put it over. They pay fine salaries, have good advertising men but they cannot sell the space in sufficient quantities to make it a paying proposition. There are many fine features in the Boston American daily and Sunday; there is no question but they are the products of brilliant minds, but enough of other matter which is very objectionable to people who have ideals, make this newspaper impossible. I remember going over this matter with Edgar L. Shaw, a fine gentleman, who was the publisher of the American at that time. I was very fond of him and he was of me, and I told him just how I felt about his paper and said that he would never be able to put it over until he was able to make changes in the news stories. I said if a salesman for bread, or shoes or any other product reports to his sales manager that the product is wrong, the manufacturer of these products tries to change it to meet the public taste, but New York insists on Boston taking what they think is good for it.

Bennett of the New York Herald told one of his directors when he was in Paris to come to Boston to hire me as advertising manager of the Herald. I will never forget the day I got a wire from him to meet him in New London. Mary was on the operating table in a hospital and I was waiting to know whether the news would be the worst or the best. The next day I met Flaherty of the New York Herald in New London and he said he had been telling Bennett all about me and Bennett said to hire me at $10,000 a year. I refused to go and they made the offer two or three times afterward, but I refused. The last time I offered to go if they would give me $15,000. Bennett was in Newport and they would wire me inside of twenty-four hours. The wire has not reached me yet and that is nineteen years ago. I was afraid to work for Bennett. He had fired too many people by telegraph and I had made up my mind to work only for white people hereafter.

It is odd how a little event shapes the current of a man's life as the pebble shapes the course of a stream. We had in our office in the early days Murray Purvies, later on the Red Book. Mr. Mathews represented the Red Book, Blue Book and Green Book in its early days and he took Murray out of express office, gave him a sales talk and sent him forth to conquer or die. Murray made a fine showing, so that in the years afterward when they took the magazine away from

Mr. Mathews they also took Murray. I met him on the street one day and he said, "Dave, you are wasting your talent. You ought to be writing letters for some great business house." I said, "Yes, Murray, just what house?" "Well," he said, "there is the John Hancock Life Insurance, a great house, and have five thousand salesmen. I know Mr. Crocker, the president, and I will give you a letter of introduction to him." I told him that would not be necessary, so I went back to the office and wrote a letter to Mr. Crocker that I had met his friend Murray Purvies, a gentleman and a sportsman, advertising man and all around good fellow, and what Murray had said to me, and this I filled in with a selling talk all about myself and what I could do for their great organization. I received an invitation to call. They were very nice and polite, but I thought a little cold toward me and my proposition, and I wrote again the next day outlining specifically my plan, proposing thirty letters, and gave the topic matter of each letter; then I got a very warm invitation from Mr. Brock, the vice president in charge of sales. He said to me, "Mr. Lawlor, we got your letter and we marvelled at it; how any man outside of the insurance business could have written that we don't know. Your offer looks awfully good to us to write these thirty letters at $60 a letter and we will give it consideration." I expected favorable results from that proposition, so I sent a carbon of the letter to my friend Tom Cummings, a librarian in Cambridge. I said, "Look this over and tell me what books I ought to read to make a good job of this." He laid out about twenty books, six or eight of them being on insurance, which could be taken up I thought when I got to that part, but the main thing being the character building of their five thousand salesmen. I was familiar more or less with all the others excepting one on the mind by Dr. Barrett and one on the body by Dr. Oppenheim. These I put in my pocket and took home and mastered their contents.

The Boston manager of the Armour plant came in a few days afterward to see our Mr. Foster to suggest a speaker for their annual dinner, and Foster told him about me and my work and said I would do a fine job for them. He gave him my scrap book, my letter to Pape, a message to employers and employees. This had been published in a national magazine and it had been favorably received not only in New England but along the line where there were newspapers and newspaper men. In addition to that there was some other matter, spiritual talks and business talks, and he told Mr. Foster that they would be very glad to have me. I refused to do it. I told Foster I was too busy, so Mr. Mathews came to me and said, "Dave, these people are our biggest customers; if you can, I would like you to make this talk for them." I told J. M., as he was familiarly called in the office, that I would do anything in the world for him, but I was not feeling too well and I was doing three or four jobs and felt this was an added burden. Then the sales manager and his assistant came to see me and I was insistent that I could not do it. But the sales manager appealed to me and said, "Here you are, a man of the world; you have traveled a lot, so why don't you give these boys a half-hour talk, because it will be a help to them. Surely you would help nearly a hundred boys and it would only take one-half an hour of your time." This was Monday and the talk was Wednesday.

The dinner was at six o'clock, so at five I went down to old St. Mary's and lit a candle and asked the help of Our Lady to do the boys some good. I discovered at the dinner the name of the club was the Armour Oval Label Club and this suggested as introduction the Oval of Light which surrounds the Virgin and her Son in the painting known as the Madonna Gonzaga by Raphael. I gave Father George of the Monastery the manuscript of this talk and asked him to look it over and see if the philosophy was all right. At that time I was president of the Laymen's Retreat Guild. The following Sunday he said that it was a fine talk and the next Sunday he said it was a very fine talk, and the third Sunday he said it was a great talk and should be published. I took no steps toward printing it, but a few months later he told me I was committing a sin by not publishing it. I explained I had no money and he said that if I had it printed he would sell it from one dollar to five dollars a copy, depending on the financial means of those who had it. He said he had been having this talk read at every retreat because after the Saturday luncheon the talk was on the will, that nothing could be done without a man willing it, and that this address of mine covered the subject, and he never missed having it read to those who assembled around the table. I mentioned the matter to Mr. Mathews. He said, "Dave, get it printed; tell on the title page it was printed for Father George of the St. Gabriel's Monastery and send me the bill."

This address was read at retreats for more than five years, until Father George was sent to some other part of the Lord's Vineyard. While it was in manuscript I took a copy to Rev. Mark C. Driscoll, D.D., the editor of the Pilot. I had never met him, but if the story interested him I would like to have it published in the Pilot. He came out to the house and he and Mary and I chatted from seven-thirty to eleven-thirty. Then he said, "Mrs. Lawlor, I have asked your good husband to come and work on the Pilot, and I cannot get a yes or a no from him." This was seventeen years ago, and it led to my working on the Pilot, which is still going on and the proceeds of which have kept the wheels of life going round and round.

I have had many wonderful experiences on the Pilot, made hundreds of delightful friends in a business way and somewhere else in this narrative I will tell of these men and those things from the Pilot which I would never have made a connection with only for "My Master's House." It brought me a trip around this great country of ours which I will tell you about as I go along, so I feel the one half-hour I gave to the boys of the Armour Oval Label Club has amply rewarded me. Armour was going to buy fifteen thousand copies of the address but the war upset their business and the deal fell through.

Quite a few of my friends bought lots of one hundred copies of "A Letter to Pape" and "My Master's House" to give to their friends. A. H. Hathaway, the baker, had me mail a copy of "A Letter to Pape" to his one hundred salesmen and said to send the bill to him. The John Hancock Insurance Company paid me $400 for the right to republish both of these in their Agency Items which went to their five thousand salesmen.

I was asked to make a communion breakfast talk in Winthrop to a council of K. of C. There were about four hundred fine men present at the breakfast, and about fifty pretty young women from one of the sodalities who waited on the tables. It seems to me in church social affairs there are too many stag parties, and many fine men and women live in single blessedness because they do not have an opportunity to meet those that they could go with hand in hand through life.

I took these men and women for a spiritual ramble and showed them some of the charities of the Catholic Church, the greatest mother in the world. I brought them to the house of the Little Sisters of the Poor, where a miracle happens every day, to the Holy Ghost Hospital for Incurables, St. Mary's Infant Asylum, the Home for Destitute Catholic Children, the House of the Good Shepherd, St. Elizabeth's Hospital, St. Joseph's Convent, the Passionist Monastery, the Seminary and our Working Boys Home, where we heard the vesper bells ringing, Boston College and Catholic education, and on our way I told the story of the missionaries and brought them into the evening office of the Church and left them at the feet of our Saviour.

It was good seed to sow. How much of it was fruitful God only knows. During the talk I explained that I was not very well and my good wife allowed me to give the talk on condition that I raised $50.00 for the Working Boys Home, which was in dire need. One of God's noblemen poor in purse, but possessing vast spiritual riches, pledged himself to send at least fifty dollars every year for the Working Boys Home. Every Christmas Eve for eighteen years there has come a Special Delivery letter to Mary with at least fifty dollars in it. One year it was ninety-seven dollars—the lowest amount was fifty-three dollars. With it comes a list of subscriptions, for this good man goes among his friends and raises this amount. His own name, like that of Abou Ben Adhem, leads all the rest. This man is like myself a salesman. I wonder if those he calls upon knows how well he stands with God.

One of my other activities with the Mathews organization was selling painted bulletins for the John Donnelly Company. This connection came about through my solicitation for Printers Ink. I tried many times to sell him, but he was what the boys call a hard-boiled egg. He suggested that the Poster Association of New England ought to advertise in Printers Ink and that the National Association should do likewise, and that he was a director of the National Organization and if I would draw up a plan he would be glad to present it. I did draw up this plan.

Mr. Foster aided me in the work with his great knowledge and ability and it was a well-done job. Mr. Foster thought we ought to get a thousand dollars from the national association for this plan, which not only included double-page spread in Printers Ink in color, but went into sales matters deeply.

One day at lunch Mr. Donnelly passed my table and I asked, "Say, when am I going to get any business from that poster association of yours?" "They are meeting at the hotel now; why don't you address them?" he answered. So at two o'clock I met seventy-five or a hundred men who owned the various outdoor plants throughout New England. I gave them what I thought was a pretty nice talk. Then the question period arose. I was only asked one question, and that by Mr. Donnelly. He said, "Mr. Lawlor, you have been selling advertising for twenty-five years or more?" I said, "Yes." "Well," he said, "you must have met many men whom you could not sell." "Why," I said laughingly, "I have met a great many men, but in all those cities there was just one man I never could get a dollar's worth of business from, and his name was E. C. Donnelly." They say the shot fired at Concord was heard round the world. I heard this story everywhere I went; I even got it in New York the next day. Somebody must have wired it.

A day or two afterward I met Mr. Donnelly on the street. He must have been a good sport, because he said, "Why don't you come to work for me?" I told him I had a job, but would make a part-time arrangement. He then agreed to pay me fifty dollars a week for part-time. The understanding was that I was to give him Monday, Tuesday and Wednesday. Of course I arranged my business so he got a part of every day in the week instead of all three days.

The advertising manager of the Record was a Dr. Ellis. He was a graduate of Harvard College. He had been city editor and advertising manager of the Herald-Traveler. He was telling me his troubles the week before with the R. H. White Company. I suggested a letter along the lines of the one I had written for the Traveler and it brought forth good results, so he gave me a five-thousand dollar order for painted bulletins in return for what I had done for him.

While I worked for Donnelly, I learned that men didn't know what they wanted to buy. They may go out to buy boards and buy posters, and they may go out to buy posters and buy paint, so I decided that if a man didn't want what I showed him I would show him something else. One of my customers was A. H. Hathaway of the Hathaway Bakeries. He is a gentleman, there are few people I like better, and I put him on my gilt edge list of friends. You know there are degrees of friends same as the weather, some are hot, some are cold and some are medium. We had been out to see some painted bulletins, but nothing suited him. I asked him to go to lunch with me and we walked down through the Common. I pointed up to the Walker Building and said, "There is what you ought to have—that wonderfully spectacular advertisement." It was just after the war and none of Mr.

Donnelly's speculators were working and all were eating their heads off. He said, "That isn't bad—what do you get for it?" I said, "$8400 a year." I then said, "I suppose you would be glad to have an artist make a sketch." He said he would, so I said, "A. H., what have you in mind to put on?" He said, "Our toast." Sketches were made and approved. I brought in Hathaway's contract one day, and Donnelly said, "Let me see it?" He examined it, no tail to it, and said, "That sure is great—go out and sell the others." Hathaway stayed on the Walker Building for three years, and then went out because Mr. Donnelly lost the location.

One of the biggest buyers of painted bulletins was Eugene M. McSweeney. He is a man of vision and a great advertising man. He was a great circulation man and later became co-publisher of the American. He selected good positions for the bulletins on the main arteries of travel in and around Boston. He knew the value of city circulation to advertisers.

It was a pleasure to do business with this cultured gentleman. He later became Fire Commissioner and is now Police Commissioner for the city of Boston, where his rare executive ability and his kindly disposition have endeared him to his men. The city's welfare is his first thought and he has already made a creditable record as commissioner.

Looking through the Herald I saw the little ad of a lumber man named Downes, so I made a call and inquired for Mr. Downes. The clerk looked at me and pointed at the sign over his desk reading "Salesmen not seen in the afternoon." "Well," I said, "I am not a salesman." "Oh," he said, "Mr. Downes is out on the wharf." Then I added, "At least the boss says I'm not." He said, "Maybe the boss is right."

Downes' order for painted bulletins was $5,000. This he increased until he became the biggest local customer on the Donnelly list.

J. Edward Downes is very likeable. He gives every man a hearing. When you call on him at his office, there are usually half a dozen salesmen sitting in groups waiting their turn, much like going to confession. He never hurries a man. He is kind and patient, and if he can't buy from you he will give you a valid reason.

It seems to me the bigger the executive is the kinder he is, at least that has been my experience in meeting buyers for the last fifty years from here to Chicago.

One bank man told me if he had his way he would tear down and burn every sign in Boston.

I asked him if he ever read Cardinal Newman's great classic, "The Present Position of the Catholic Church in England." He confessed he had not. I suggested that he do so, as there was a very fine story there which showed that there were two medallions on the monument, one gold and one silver. There are two sides to everything, and he should see the Donnelly side.

Another Boston merchant believed in outdoor advertising, but his father did not, and would be displeased if he used outdoor advertising. But I said, "Your father's dead." "Yes," he said, "but he would not like it."

I wrote many letters to advertisers for C. T. Donnelly. They bore his signature, but he never saw them until he heard from them. One was to a Boston merchant, A. Shuman, about a choice location we had on Commonwealth Avenue. It was a two-page letter, and after describing the location and the circulation it gave, there was a short essay on the law of sale.

This letter was mailed in the morning, the merchant received it in the afternoon, he and his wife went to see the location in the evening. He called up the advertising manager at his home and instructed him to be at Donnelly's office in the morning when it opened and buy the sign at the price it was offered—$1200.

There was much prejudice against painted signs twenty years ago, when I started selling for Donnelly, but that has about disappeared. The outdoor operator has done his share. He does not erect in residential districts or beauty spots, being a lover of the beautiful himself.

One day going by a great Boston establishment, S. S. Pierce Company, Charlie Donnelly said, "I have had a salesman call on the advertising manager every week for seven years, and he never got an order." "He is calling on the wrong man, Charlie," I said, "he should see the boss."

"You see him, Dave," said Charlie, with a twinkle in his eye. "I wrote a letter to the owner about his store and the excellence of his goods and mentioned a particular item that should be advertised very profitably on a new location on Commonwealth Avenue." The next day Charlie got a phone call from the advertising manager. The boss wanted to see him that morning at his convenience. We both went to see the gentleman. He gave us cigars. We had a brief talk and drove out to the location, which he purchased immediately at $1500 a year.

The point of this story is "See the right man, but if you can't see him write him and have the letter bear the signature of the big man of your concern."

Big men want to talk to big men. I remember an advertising manager calling on the head of a big store. He said, "Mr. Munsey sent me over to tell you about the Journal." "You tell my advertising manager your message. If Mr. Munsey has anything to say to me, he can come and see me and I will talk to him," and that ended the interview.

I wrote this same merchant five letters from the Traveler, but they bore the publisher's signature, and Baker got the business. Letters are great business-getters if they carry a good story and reach the right man.

As an advertising man, I would say posters and painted signs have their place; if a man knows how to use them they will give him business at a profit.

E. C. Donnelly has been called to his Maker, but in his hands were many good deeds.

He was a genius as a builder. When he succeeded his father some fifty years ago his inheritance was not much more than a bucket of paste and a brush. When his book was closed he owned nearly every plant from Portland, Maine down to Springfield, Mass. The total value would be between three and four millions of dollars. His brother Charles E. was sales manager, a very likeable, lovable man. He came to see me most every day and a hundred times I rode the plant with him.

I continued this part-time with E. C. Donnelly for ten years, resigning on my 60th birthday. E. C. would have been a success in any business. He had a great brain and a lot of courage. He was apt to become irritated when a little thing was not properly done. Big things might go wrong that might mean a great loss, but he kept on smiling. He was a good paymaster. The money was always ready on pay day.

I believe he did more for outdoor advertising than anyone in the business, with the possible exception of Cusack of Chicago, who had a greater field. Donnelly bought the best locations and his painted bulletins were works of art.

His son, E. C. Donnelly Jr., is now head of the business and doing very well. Under his direction the firm has built a great many beautiful Neon signs for the business men of greater Boston.

Mathews said once upon a time that if there was any impossible thing to do to give it to Dave, he will find some man for whom he has done a kind act who will sit up all night to put over a deal for him.

Our Chicago representative wired the office one day that the Ward's Orange Crush advertising had been ordered taken from the Worcester Gazette and given to the Post of that city. The wire explained that this was done by orders of the advertiser and he did it at the request of his Worcester distributor. Mr. Mathews and Mr. Foster were much disturbed about this. The Gazette was one of their star papers and the agency worked for star papers day and night. These papers paid the office large sums of money in commissions and they expected the advertising for their papers. Here was an odd situation. The distributor was hostile to the Gazette because of an attack they made on him when he was a brewer. He would not see any one from the Gazette office or any one representing the Gazette, so the matter looked hopeless. Foster stated the situation to me, saying that as this man was of my faith maybe I could do something with him. It was work outside my department, but the interest of the office always came first to me. Foster drove me down to Worcester but the distributor was away, so I decided to stay all night. In the afternoon I got back to the office and told Mathews everything was O. K., that the Gazette would hold the business. He wanted to know how I did it and I told him it was very simple. I called up my old friend Bill Brennan, advertising manager of the Gazette, and told him what was in the works. Brennan said to me, "Dave, this man is my intimate personal friend. I will fix things for you. I would not lift a finger to help Mathews nor would I move an inch to help George Booth of the Gazette, but I owe this to you, for when I was down and out and no one would give me a job it was your recommendation that led Tobey to give me a fine job on the American." Bill Brennan called his friend's house every hour until he found him at two o'clock in the morning and arranged for him to give me an interview.

I took Mary and David on many of my business trips. Even when Mary could not go I took David from the time he was five until he was nine, when he decided he had seen about all of New England and New York City. One day when David was about seven, we went in to see John F. Ratham of the Journal Bulletin of Providence. Ratham said, "Hello, David, how are things?" and David replied, "They would be better if you gave us a page for Printers Ink." "That is crude," said Ratham. "Your father is not bringing you up right. Sit in my chair and let me show you how to do it." He walked to the end of his office about twenty feet away and walked to where we were and said, "Good morning, Mr. Lawlor, it is a beautiful day, I hope you are feeling very well." David waved his little hand and said, "If you are going to talk about Printers Ink I tell you now there is nothing doing."

Ratham was the most embarrassed man I ever saw, and then he roared with laughter. "So that is how they use your dad, is it?" he said. He handed me a page and I saw that it was important and asked for two pages. He would not give them to me. David opened the Saturday Post and showed him a two-page spread. Still he would not give in, but as we were going out the door he called David and handed him a note. I read, "You win, kid, tell dad to make it two pages." He always inquired for the boy and said that any time I would send him alone he would give him a page or two, but I said not for the whole of his plant and Printers Ink would I send him alone.

The office paid my expenses but I always lost money on these trips. The expense account showed transportation and hotel, but every man on the road will tell you that they lose money on every trip. There are little expenses here and there that are never put on the expense list.

I made three or four calls on Frank P. Bennett of the Cotton and Wool Reporter, a high grade textile weekly. Bennett was president of the State Senate and he was a very able man.

One Monday morning I dropped in in the interest of Printers Ink. "Did you go to church Sunday," I asked Mr. Bennett.

He said, "I did not. My wife chided me on her return from church, and I told her that I had read a better sermon than our minister ever delivered."

"So," I said, "you too believe God is helping those who are doing His work, and is eliminating those who are working against Him."

"Sure I believe it," said he, "and you read that story in the Saturday Evening Post. It was great, and the lesson is true though the characters are probably fictitious. Now, Mr. Lawlor, I like you, I like your style, your address and your philosophy. I would like to chat with you often. I will make a contract with you for 52 issues of Printers Ink, that will be

$2,080, but it must be a condition of the contract that you visit me every week for a year."

I declined the contract under these conditions so we compromised on a visit every month and so it was written in the contract. Bennett kept his contract and I enjoyed keeping mine. Selling advertising is more than quoting rates and circulation.

Mr. Mathews came into my office one day with a copy of the Boston Globe containing a half-page advertisement of the Foster Rubber Heel Company.

"Dave," he said, "this is outside your department, but I would like you to get an order to run this advertising in our thirty-eight newspapers exclusively in our cities. We will give the advertiser cooperation, we will send a letter to every cobbler and shoe dealer in all our cities. The cost of this advertising for one time is $2500 and I will give you a commission of ten per cent if you make the sale." As he passed my office a few hours later he stopped and looked inquiringly. I held up two fingers. "You sold it for two insertions, Dave, that is great. Tell Miss Lang to make out a check for you for $500." Then he added, "I knew you were the only one in this organization who could put that over." Mathews had noticed some weeks before that I had done a nice piece of work for a man who could reward me by giving me the business. While the order was for two times the advertiser ran six times and J. M. paid the bonuses every time without a murmur.

My friend Frank Baker after the merging of the Herald-Traveler came to see me and said, "Dave, I can get a job on the Herald, but at the end of ten years I will still have a job. I am not going to be a hind tit so I am going to look for a little paper somewhere and be a publisher again." He found it in

Tacoma, Washington, and every year when he came east to publisher's convention I used to meet him and discuss with him his problems, his hopes and his fears. He wanted Charlie Welsh, the editor of the Traveler, to go with him to Tacoma, but they could not come to an agreement on salary. They both agreed that they would leave the matter with me and I set Charlie Welsh's salary for five years. Each year showed an increase and the last two years gave him a percentage of the profits, if any.

Senator Perkins owned the great daily in Tacoma and he was a power in the business world as well as that of politics. Frank Baker kept digging away making increases. One day he bought all Perkins' holdings in his morning and evening newspaper, combined his own with them, and since that time Frank has been riding on top of the world. It was a well-deserved success. I never met a squarer man. He was honest with his readers and honest with his advertisers, and he loves Tacoma. In addition to his newspapers he has many other interests. I met him in New York at the publisher's convention in 1920. He came to my room and I gave him a copy of "My Master's House" to read, while I was preparing to go to lunch with him. After reading it he said, "Dave, put your autograph on that, it is beautiful. I'd like to have you and Mrs. Lawlor come out to Tacoma to see me. There are some letters I want you to write and you ought to see this fine city and know conditions. I will give you $1,000 for your expenses and I will give you $2,000 more for the letters I want you to write. So in August Mary and I left for California. As I was not very well, we planned to stop off at Chicago and Denver, the Grand Canyon, Los Angeles, and stay a week in San Francisco, where Mary had a lot of cousins, then spend a week in Tacoma with Frank Baker and come home via Vancouver and the Canadian Rockies.

When we got to Denver, we found there was a car strike. Every street car in the whole city was tied up and the conductors and motormen were in a fighting condition. The city was in a turmoil. We were refused a room at the Brown's Palace Hotel because people who lived at some little distance had stayed at the hotel since they couldn't get home. I insisted in a nice way that I must have a room, and the clerk told me he had turned two hundred and fifty people away since two o'clock. I smiled at him and said, "Now here, is it fair to turn a man of my age out with two hundred and fifty people ahead of me? What chance have I got in this town, no cars running, you can hardly get a cab for love or money. Don't you think there is a room somewhere in this hotel?" I think it was Mary's smile that won him, for he said, "I can get you a room for twenty dollars," and I laid down the twenty dollars. I don't think he took advantage of me, for it was the most wonderful room I ever saw, in fact it was a small suite. Sorry we didn't have a chance to see Denver, though.

We went to Colorado Springs and saw the beauties in that fine place, then on to the Grand Canyon, the greatest wonder in the world. We spent the entire day there. I wish we could have spent a month. It was truly magnificent in its splendor but what impressed me was the great silence of the place. It seemed to speak of eternity. The morning after we left Williams I saw for the first time the power of water. There had been a cloud burst on the road and the water had rushed down and torn up the track for a distance of four miles. The double track stood up straight like a fence for the entire distance. We were delayed some six or eight hours, at the edge of the desert, until repairs were made, then on to the Needles, where I believe it was one hundred and twenty degrees in the shade. My physician had advised me when I got to town not to ride anywhere but to sit on the piazza and rest. A friend met us at the hotel in Los Angeles and invited us out for a little ride and we covered sixteen cities and towns that surround Los Angeles. He took us a distance of ninety-six miles and I never saw a more beautiful place than this city of Angels in Southern California. Mary's relatives came to California some thirty-five or forty years ago, so they showed us many of the things worth seeing, and there are a lot of them. So we saw San Francisco and the cities and towns that surround for fifty miles. Mary said, "Dave, we won't say anything to David about this until after he has left college, because if he ever comes out to see this wonderful place we will never get him to finish his college course." We stopped off in Portland and went down the Columbia highway and saw the statues erected to Clark and Lewis. The view from this superb statue looking over into the State of Washington is superb.

Charlie Welsh and his good wife were our entertainers in Tacoma, because Frank had gone to Alaska and would not be back for three or four days. Charlie drove us all over this fine city and entertained us at his home, and then we decided to go over to Seattle for a day. I said to Mary, "There was a boy I knew in Fall River came out here and is in one of the stores." Inquiring in the personnel department of the Bon Marche, the biggest store there, if there was a Mr. Frank McDermott connected with the store, the girl opened her eyes in surprise and said, "He is the sole owner." Frank put his arms around me and said, "Dave, my best friend, and I have not seen you for thirty years." I said, "That is true, Frank, have you kept the faith?" He said, "I will show you. For two years I gave up this business and went to France as an unpaid secretary for the Knights of Columbus. But come out to the house and then we will go out to our country home, 'Faraway.' " He had the most beautiful house that I have ever seen. He told me he had purchased it at a greatly reduced price from some very rich man. He said it was almost dishonest to buy this little place for a little over a quarter of a million. We then went down to his country home, sixty miles from Seattle down the Puget Sound, right into the heart of the primeval forest.

He said, "I have given you the fastest ride you have ever had in your life on the water because there is nothing built that can go as fast as this boat can." The boat surely did fly. His country home is known as the show place of the Northwest. There are about fifty acres of land and a beautiful house. The living room must be about fifty feet by thirty, has a huge fireplace, and around it are trophies of game that Mr. McDermott had won in his hunting expeditions. There were tennis courts and a swimming pool and everything to be desired to make life a round of pleasure. A remarkable thing—none of the windows had screens and he told me that the fly and the mosquito are unknown there. Every evening a pile of logs six feet high are set afire by everyone who lives along the Sound and the families gather each around his own fire and play the fiddle or concertina with much dancing and merriment. This beautiful picture I believe I never will forget. We were in the living room one evening when the clock struck nine. Mr. McDermott arose and said,

"My friends, it has always been the custom in my house at nine o'clock to say the Rosary of the Blessed Virgin. I would be pleased to have all who would care to join me in prayer." And he knelt down and said the Rosary aloud. This was a magnificent profession of his faith, for many of his guests were not only Catholics and Protestants, but maybe some who had no belief. He showed me afterward a table which he opened up and it was an altar. He said some few months before a bishop celebrated mass in this living room and after the mass walked through the grounds with another bishop who was also present. He told me Mrs. McDermott, who had been his lifetime partner, had a little while before gone to heaven, but her gifts to charity were so great that these two dignitaries of the church showed their appreciation by coming out into the wilderness to offer, in what had been her home, prayers for her eternal happiness.

I left this place with a great deal of regret after a stay of several days. Mr. Baker had gotten home in the meantime and of course didn't know where we were. There was no way of notifying my friends where we were because Faraway was without any means of communication. When you were there you were really far away from the world. After talking matters over with Frank we went on to Seattle and Vancouver. I watched the Canadian Rockies from four o'clock in the morning until noon. I am not going to attempt to describe them, as that is beyond me, but the thought came to me, as the great scientists figured that the depth of the Grand Canyon was caused by erosion of the Colorado River that they were wrong, that it was there the Almighty dipped his hand and took out enough material to build the Rocky Mountains.

We stopped over at Winnipeg to break the journey, then on to Minneapolis. I thought I would like to see the Journal office, because that was where I was to be advertising manager when Swift hired me some twenty years before. Here I met my old friend Gerald Pierce, who was advertising manager. He had left the Record Herald and come on to the Journal, made his pile, told me he was going to Florida to live and spend the remainder of his day. I remember the day he said, "I think I will live longer with a book and a pipe, sitting in the shade of an orange tree, than I will up in this climate where it goes to twenty or thirty below zero." He had his chauffeur show us the beautiful lakes that surround Minneapolis, and they are gorgeous, and then took us down to the Cathedral in St. Paul which I had long desired to visit.

Mary tells her friends that no matter where we go she finds one of Dave's friends who has a car and wants to show us around. I have tried to make friends and I have tried to keep the friends I make. Kindly acts are what make friends and to keep them is to always look at their virtues and never chide them on their weaknesses. We passed Milwaukee on our way home. I used to run up there looking for business from the breweries. They had so many that it was known as the beer city. Schlitz and Pabst and other great names in the advertising world had their works in the city. When Volstead put breweries on the retired list the city felt it would hardly ever recover, but Palmolive Soap and its products I believe have a greater volume of business than was ever enjoyed by all the breweries in Milwaukee. We didn't stop in Chicago on the way back because after an absence of some time there comes a heart-hunger to see the faces of the loved ones. We had been gone a little over six weeks, and of course I expected no salary from Donnelly, for nothing had been done in that time, but I found my six weeks' back wage awaiting me, and ever since that time I have said many a prayer for E. C. Donnelly.

While I never was able to give much money to charity or good causes, I always gave something. I have secured positions for quite a number of men and women and girls and boys who have come to me when they could not find work. This was not only true in the Mathews' office but in the Pilot. Father Driscoll used to say, "Dave, you will not get money for the time and labor you have spent in securing those, but you will get your pay some other way. 'Who does God's work will get God's pay.'" I met in an agency one day a very fine gentleman who attracted me very much and I invited him to visit me at my office. We went out to luncheon several days and I learned from him that he was a protegee of the Archbishop Williams, formerly head of the Boston archdiocese. The good Archbishop sent this boy to St. Charles School at Baltimore, having seen in him all the qualities for the priesthood. Then he sent him to the Sorbonne in Paris and to Rome, where he studied for some time. He had a vocation for the priesthood, but circumstances arose for him to have to go out in the world and earn a living for his father and mother. He was in the Boston Public Library for some years, then became secretary to the brilliant John Boyle O'Reilly, who was then editor of the Pilot. Cummings was business manager from five to six years and on his return from a trip in Europe he found that O'Reilly had died and was lying side by side in the same tomb with Cummings' own boy, who had died about the same time. Cummings was the founder of the Knights of Columbus Journal "Columbia," and he had a great deal to do with the spread of the great organization. It was he who got permission from the Archbishops of New York and Baltimore and Chicago to establish councils in their dioceses. Then he had become a lecturer and derived his income from giving lectures on Art and Literature. War broke out and his income suddenly stopped. He was an officer in one of the military organizations, and I believe he was assigned to care for the docks in Charlestown.

He came in one day and said, "I have applied for a position as librarian in a cantonment in France." I said, "Tom, you are too old for that. You are approaching sixty. It is a long journey and a hard life." "Well," he said, "I must live; I have no money and I have a little family. Here is the letter I am sending to the librarian at Congress asking for the position." It was a very good letter. I said, "Tom, instead of sending that to Washington, send it to the seven trustees of the library at Cambridge." He said, "Why, there is no opening."

I said, "I know there is going to be a change there and you call them up after they have had a chance to read your letter." A couple of days later he said, "I have called on all these men and I think my chances are pretty good, but I met an old friend of mine and he said, 'You haven't a Chinaman's chance. There are forty-three men all looking for that job and they all have friends.'" I said, "Tom, none have the training that you have and I think you will get that job." In about a week he came around to me. He said, "Two of the trustees don't like me; one objects to my collar, which is soft, and the other does not like my tie, it is cheap."

We had lunch together, and I said, "Here you buy

an E. & W. collar, then you buy a handsome tie, then you go to see those men. You say to the man who objected to your collar, 'I know you are with me, do you know that anyone is against me?' and say the same thing to the one who objects to your tie."

The next day the trustees met and Tom got the vote of every one of them. He stayed there about ten years and was appointed librarian of the City of Fall River and made a great hit in my old home town, but the Good Lord thought that he had worked enough and he called him to his reward. Among the few paintings I have in my house is the Infant on the Cross. It was brought to me by Cummings on the twenty-fifth anniversay of our marriage. He said, "Dave, this is the most valuable thing I own and I want you to take it as a reward for the good things you have done for me."

The only time I ever spoke of money to Mr. Mathews was when I was with him ten years. I said to him, "I want to have a serious talk with you," so he said for me to come up to his club with him that night for dinner. After dinner he leaned back and said, "What is it?" I said, "When I came to you ten years ago I was broke, and after ten years working for you I am still broke; what are you going to do about it, what does the future hold?" He said, "Dave, in the ten years you have been with me, you have made a thousand friends, you have become a cultivated gentleman, you have read a great deal so that you are well informed on almost every subject, and in the eyes of the world you are an educated man."

"What have I got out of the business, just a few dollars." I looked at him, but he continued. "But I will increase your drawing account $1,000 a year and I will loan you sufficient money to put you on easy street." This is the only time we ever discussed money. When I was finishing fourteen years with Mr. Mathews I had been rejected in life insurance on account of high blood pressure. I went to see my doctor about it and he asked me how long I had been working and I told him forty-nine years. I told him what my duties were, I represented the Julius Mathews Special Agency and my work carried me all over New England, and that I had traveled about 60,000 miles for the firm and I usually sat in the smoker and played auction pitch to improve my mind. I represented Printers Ink and this led me to do business with all the publishers in New England and it was some tough job, and that I worked for the Boston suburban newspapers and that I worked for John Donnelly & Sons, and my job was to sell advertising, mostly painted bulletins to a lot of people who hated boards and who told me if they had their way they would tear them down. In addition to that I was selling for the Boston Pilot, which he knew all about and which was the great Catholic newspaper in Boston.

I told him that was about all the work I did weekdays, but Sundays I usually went up to St. Gabriel's monastery, made a talk to the boys who were on retreat and I had been doing this twenty-five times a year for the last four years. Then in the evening I usually have four or five or six friends come into the house and we play forty-fives with a group of men who are gardeners and laborers and some other evening in the same week we play bridge with doctors and lawyers and clergymen and men of affairs, so I said, as we say in confession, "that is about all I can remember." He said, "Don't you think it about time you took a rest? The old engine has been going for forty-nine years, you cannot go on forever, better rest up. Now

I am going to give you a diet and some medicine and I want you to take things very easy."

The next morning we got a letter from Printers Ink which required a call on the Springfield Republican and I made a trip and found that Liggett had just bought the building and had taken out, in process of remodelling, the stairways and the elevators. So I phoned up to the Republican and found my man and asked him to lunch. He said if I wanted to see him I would have to come up and I explained about the stairway and the elevator. He told me that he climbed the fire escape to the fifth story and if I wanted to see him I could climb the fire escape. I climbed five floors on the fire escape, found I was a story too high, came down and went in to see him. He did have the grace to apologize, saying he never realized my age, and that he had had mince pie the night before and was not feeling well, and it would never happen again. I didn't tell either Mr. Mathews or Mary about this trip, just waited to see what would happen. Then came the notice from Printers Ink discontinuing our services.

Mr. Mathews said that my drawing account of $3000 a year was coming from Printers Ink and that he would discontinue it. Then he said that Fahey had made a contract with him for representing the Worcester Post and he would allow me $300 for this as it was my department. I thanked him. "Will I give you $60 a week for five weeks out of this money or will I let it apply on your house account?" he asked. "Let it apply on the house account," I replied. "How will you live, Dave?" he asked. "I will live all right," I said.

The daily newspapers that I made contracts with for Julius Mathews' service during my fourteen years of active service paid Mr. Mathews about $50,000 a year, or in the aggregate about three-quarters of a million dollars. I go to see him every couple of weeks, and at Christmas time I give him a book and he gives me a couple of gold pieces as he gives all his employees. I have always had the kindliest feeling towards Mr. Mathews. He has a great agency. Mr. Foster is now the general manager, and he sees to it that every publisher gets everything that belongs to him plus a little more. In my time they took only New England cities, but now the headquarters have been moved to New York and they are taking newspapers in various sections of the country. I don't think that I ever saw Mr. Mathews idle for a moment, a slow worker but a very careful one, almost microscopic. I told him he weighed things on a jeweler's scale while I weighed things on a hay scale, meaning that he was more accurate than I. Then he said to me, "Dave, that is all right to say, but when it is necessary I find you use the jeweler's scale."

The great strength of his agency is the persistent pursuit of the advertiser as well as his advertising agent. They gave the advertiser no rest until they were in the columns of the paper they represented. While their men visit the agencies, keep in touch and contact with those who hand it out, the advertiser who pays the bills is being told about the publications that are on Mathews' list. Mr. Mathews knows men and life pretty well. In his early days he was a shoe salesman, traveled all over the country, and so he knows the law of sales. He knows you must have the product so he usually picks the best paper in a place. He knows he must advertise it, so he is continually advertising what he represents. With the money he made in the shoe business he went into some Southern enterprise and he said that at one time if a man offered to insure his becoming a millionaire and the price was $1.00 he would refuse to take it, he was so sure of his million. A little while later he lost everything except his wife. Later he came to Boston and a friend loaned him a desk. There was to be no rent for six months and he walked three miles every day to save carefare and he knew the value of a dollar. He used to say, "Dave, if you want to know the value of $100 just try to get a loan." He started with the Rockland Star and then he used to write his letters in longhand to the advertiser; now I believe he has about forty newspapers and about sixty men and women to help to run the business.

Mr. Mathews is not a churchgoer, probably he has been in a church half a dozen times in fifty years, but I find that he is quite a biblical scholar. I know the divine spark burns within his breast because he told me only a little while ago that often when he finds it difficult to go to sleep he recites a little hymn that he learned at his mother's knee. He said it goes like this: "Now I lay me down to sleep and pray the Lord my soul to keep; if I should die before I wake, I pray the Lord my soul to take." I have met quite a few men who are leading good lives and have the respect of their fellow men, yet they are not churchgoers. We of the Catholic faith are bound under penalty of mortal sin from the age of seven, which is the age of reason, to attend mass on Sundays and holydays and to receive the sacraments at stated intervals. Nor are the old and infirm excused, because if they are unable to go to church the priest of the parish is bound to visit them and bring to them the Blessed Sacrament.

I could have been advertising manager of the Houghton Dutton Company Department Store.

George Dutton and Billy Freeman, my old employer on the New York American, were playing golf at Pinehurst. George asked Billy a lot of questions about retail store advertising and Billy told him to hunt up Dave Lawlor when he got back to Boston. He said, "Dave knows more about retail store advertising than I will ever know." George and his partner, Alex McGregor, offered me the place, but I was happy where I was. Then George offered to pay me $300 a year for the privilege of coming in to talk to me.

Some time ago at the City Club, which has a very good rule that all men know each other without introduction, a stranger to me asked some question that in answer I had to explain that I was a newspaper man and he asked me if I knew Williams of the Transcript. I confessed I didn't have the pleasure, and that while I knew nearly every editor and publisher in New England I had never had the pleasure of meeting Mr. Williams, who was not only an able man but a fine one too. He said the reason was that Mr. Williams was to address the Algonquin Club after church service Sunday. "That is the rich men's club?" I asked, and he said, "Yes." I asked how many of the Algonquin Club members go to church on Sunday. He said, "Damned if I know; I haven't been to church in fifty years." "Well," I said, "in fifty years I have missed church seven times due to illness or travel." "Oh," he said, "you were brought up in a small place where there was not much activity, so of course you went to church." I said, "In fifty years I have lived in Providence, Fall River, New York, Pittsburgh, Chicago and Boston. They are not all small places and I have seen people pouring into the churches at six, seven, eight and nine o'clock mass." He said, "I admit the Roman Catholic church has a hold on its people, but

I don't go to church." I said, "Well, that is all right, but those who miss going to church lose many of the fine things in life." "That may be," he said, "but I don't go and I don't intend to go." I asked, "Are you married?" He said, "Yes." I said, "You have a boy who is of marriageable age?" "No," said he, "but I have a daughter." "Well," I said, "suppose when she marries she lives in the same town and never writes you, never goes to see you, in fact passes your door without going in to see you, what would you think of that?" "That would be terrible." I said, "Well, you surely admit you had a Creator, or did you just grow like Topsy?" He bowed his head and said, "I know I had a Creator," and I said, "Your father's house is on many streets and you pass by without going in to speak to him?" He looked up in astonishment and said, "My God, who are you?" I smiled and said, "An advertising solicitor who goes into his Father's House and tells Him how he is getting along and what help he wants."

Some men tell me that they get their solace and inspiration from nature, but they don't seem to see that nature is only the hand-maiden of God and behind the flowers and the trees and the birds there is He who created them. Those who do not go to church are not going anywhere nor are they getting anywhere.

Shortly after I became a member of the Mathews' organization I moved to Oak Square, Brighton. This was the nineteenth time I had moved since I was married and led my cousin to suggest that I get a house on wheels. It seemed to me that I was everlastingly on the go. I was only there a week when a new parish was formed. Rev. Daniel W. Linnehan, now the pastor of a great church in Malden, came to us as our pastor. He came to us like the apostle of old, his fortune in his hand, but a man of wonderful faith. The only place he could get to say Mass was in a garage. After the services that night the members of the new parish held a meeting as to what was to be done and there was considerable talk but very little action.

I told the story of a friend who was going over on a ferryboat from New York to Hoboken, and a little boy, the son of a widow, fell off and got drowned. Everyone surrounded the widow and said they were sorry. My friend said, "We are all sorry, but I am sorry $20 worth, so anyone who wishes to give their sorrow concrete form can put it in this hat," so taking this lesson from my friend I told them I would put $20 in the hat and they could all show by similar action just what they want to do for this parish of ours. That little meeting, because we had the smallest parish in the diocese, gathered together $750 which was the nucleus of the parish which now has property worth $300,000 to $400,000. At the meeting the next night they made me president of the Holy Name Society and at the meeting of the women they made Mary first prefect of the Sodality of the Blessed Virgin. I only kept my place six or seven years, but Mary has rounded out the twenty-fifth year in her office.

Reverend Father Linnehan was chaplain at the Little Sisters of the Poor for some eighteen years and he saw the good things these sisters accomplished. They care for a couple of hundred old men and women. They have no money and every day they get out and beg for the things that are necessary to keep body and soul together of those helpless old people. This led to a lifetime friendship with this good priest. Mary and I helped to run his field days for ten or twelve years until the parish was on its feet financially and they were no longer necessary. Then I made a retreat at the St. Gabriel's Monastery and wrote of my experiences for the Post.

In this report I told the story of a man named Harswell, an Englishman and a friend of the faith who was a buyer at Bigelow and Kennard, one of the great jewelry houses in Boston. Harswell lived in a mill tenement in Lowell so that his salary could go to help a poor family and educate one of their sons who was blind. In the gathering at the monastery the day the paper appeared was His Eminence, the Cardinal, who told me what a wonderful story it was and gave me his blessing for writing it. Some time later Father George sent for me and said there was to be an election of officers and another gentleman present and I were to run for vice-president. I told Father George to give it to the other man as I didn't want to be other than a private in the ranks. The other man said he would like to take it as he would like the honor of being vice-president of this group of men. Father George asked me to stay and let the other go. He told me that was a test and he wanted me to be president. I refused the honor and he implored Mary to help him to make me accept the presidency of the organization. Finally I consented to be vice-president and I occupied that position for two years; the president passed away in the meantime, so I had to take the presidency. The principal duty of the office was to meet the gentlemen Sunday who had been on retreat since Friday night and tell them what was expected of them when they went out in the world to show a good example and that they were really followers of Christ.

There are twenty-five retreats a year, so for four years I had the privilege of addressing those good men, many of whom the latchets of whose shoes I was not worthy to loosen. I believe that there have been over 10,000 men who have been making retreats at this monastery. They start the retreat Friday night and end it at seven o'clock Monday morning and they go away laden with spiritual treasures. I have had the great opportunity to meet many of those wonderful men who have taken the vows of poverty, chastity and obedience. We were gathered in the library one night after being on retreat with Father Hubert, an old man who had seen the world in all its phases. He had been through the great war and had seen all kinds of sin, sorrow and suffering. We were gathered in the library, about fifty of us, when he came in to bid us good-bye, as he had a call to go to some other city. I said, "Father, may I ask you a question? I have a boy in Boston College and while the good Jesuits would like everyone to be one hundred per cent in their studies and deportment, yet no one ever gets that; but if he gets in the nineties they rate him as wonderful and if he gets in the eighties they tell him he is fine." "Yes," said the good father. I said, "He tells me that if he only gets seventy they pass him and give him their diploma." "Yes," said Father Hubert, not quite able to appreciate what I was driving at. "Well," I said, "Father, you have seen a lot of this world and you know more about our Great Teacher than we will ever know, but isn't it possible that He too will pass us if we only get seventy?" The good father said, "Boys, He will pass you if you get seventy," and he turned to the door and said, "Boys, if you get fifty, the Great Teacher will pass you," and then he went out and then opened the door again and with a wave of his hands he said, "If you get twenty-five you will be saved."

The seventeen years on the Pilot have been happy

years. This in a measure was due to the great spirituality of the head of that institution, the Reverend Mark C. Driscoll, D.D. He was the editor up to seven years ago, when he was made pastor of St. Francis de Sales Church in Charlestown. He was not only the editor but, in the language of newspaper men, he was the whole works. He had the good sense to seek advice of men who had specialized in the various departments in newspaper activities and acting on their advice, by a lot of hard work and a lot of prayer, he made the Pilot the great religious paper that it is. He is a kindly man and many a time when I was short of money he loaned me from the treasury and quite a few times from his own meager bank account.

I say he was a spiritual man because I know his life is one of almost continual prayer. We say a couple of Rosaries a day and think we are doing pretty well, while this good man not only attended activities which were necessary on a great paper like the Pilot, but he found time to say from thirty-five to forty Rosaries a day. He surrounded himself with a fine group of men and women, spiritual, able and hard workers. The men and women in his organization realized that he had a kindly interest in them and they served him faithfully. He has been succeeded as editor by his long-time assistant and friend, another good and able man, Reverend Edward M. Campbell, and later by Father Quinn.

Lunching with a mutual friend the Father said, "I often wonder where Dave gets the business that he gets, but I figure it that he prays a lot." I laughed although I didn't tell him that I had been impressed a great deal by the story of St. Thomas, who was the head of a band of mendicant friars. Father Thomas called one of the band to him one day and said, "The other members are complaining that you are not on the job, that you spend your time in the churches instead of going from house to house; how about it?" And the good man said that he could not pass his Father's House without going in and telling Him how he was doing. Father Thomas said, "My good man, there is a church on almost every corner in Rome; you must cut out this church business and get out and hustle like the other men." The good priest said, "All right, Father Thomas, I will do what you ask, but how does what I bring in compare with the others?" On looking the books over he said, "I find that you bring in three times as much as the others, so you just continue going into those churches."

Some eighteen years ago a pretty blue-eyed baby came to visit us. When she was five, I asked, "Mariam what would you ask Santa Claus for if he came to see us?"

"I would ask him for everything in his pack, Uncle Dave," she said, with a lovely smile.

"You have taught me how to pray, child," I exclaimed. "Now I will ask the Giver of Gifts for the material as well as the spiritual." And I have asked many times for many things. I have asked when so ill that the doctor looked grave and worried, when the little children of the neighborhood walked on tiptoe by the house so as not to disturb me, and when the good priest of the parish gave me the last sacraments of the Church. For there was work to be done. So I can with a grateful heart recite nightly "Te Deum Laudamus."

My work in the Pilot brought me in intimate touch with the retailers of Boston and I found them a fine lot of men with here and there an exception. The first advertisement I got for the Pilot was from my old friend Alexander McGregor, of Houghton & Dutton Company. This kindly Scotchman left the company and went into the insurance business. He gave me an eighty-dollar advertisement which was paid for by himself and not by the company. He said that he did not hear from the advertisement but at the end of the year Alexander McGregor had made more sales of insurance than any other man in the Mutual Life Insurance Company. Father Driscoll often felt that we sold more than circulation, and the same thought was expressed to me by Father Harold, the editor of the Sign.

I sold the Pilot advertising space to the President of the First National Stores and the President of the A. & P. Stores. The copy of their respective stores is in the Pilot every week.

In the archdiocese of Boston there are about 1,800,000 souls, and 1,200,000 of these are Roman Catholics, so I point out to an advertiser that the man on his right and the man on his left are Roman Catholics.

All of my customers are friends of mine. I visit them every week or two and they are all glad to see me and we talk over their business and sometimes they confide their troubles to me and I give them the best that is in me. I cannot cover the territory now like a young man, so from time to time I write and phone my friends, telling them how much good it would do them to have copy in the Pilot. We had a little Italian office boy who, after four or five years, Father Driscoll put into the composing room. I met him the other day and he said, "Well, I see that business is pretty good." I said, "Yes." He said, "Of course you are working very hard," and he laughed, "sitting at the telephone mostly?" "Well," I said, "if business is so easy to get on the telephone why don't the other boys get it that way?" and he said, "Your friends know if they don't give you the business you will tell Santa Claus on them."

We didn't have automobile advertising in the Pilot for some years, and one day Father Driscoll said to me that he had quite a few men out on this business and had sent them to Detroit and didn't seem to get anywhere, so he added the automobiles to my list. I asked my son if he wouldn't help me to cover them and he reported that he had a chat with an auto man who said unless we could get Packard and Studebaker we would not get anywhere. Dave and I called on Mr. Fuller, who was Governor of Massachusetts, and is now known as the Great Governor. I told the story of the Pilot to him, what we were doing, the message that we carried, and in a little while we got the advertising of Packard and then I went to see Joe Donovan, then the head of the Studebaker Company, who has since passed away and I hope he is in Heaven, for he was a wonderfully good man and did many fine things in his life. He seemed to be not only averse to advertising in the Pilot, but I thought a little hostile. I kept telling him about the Pilot, so in self-defense he said, "I know Father Driscoll, the editor of the Pilot." I said, "He certainly is a wonderfully able man and a very good man." He said, "I know Father Campbell, the assistant." "Then you know a good man," I added. "These men are working for the love of God, and I believe they get the whole sum of fifteen dollars a week, as they rank as curates."

"Joe," I said, "a monk found outside his poor cell a wounded canary. He nursed it back to health and then from time to time he taught it various acts until he had the most wonderful canary in the world. At his command it would turn a somersault, go up a ladder backward and do many wonderful things. The monk became very much attached to it. One day the provincial of the order visited the community and the canary was put through his act for him. The provincial said to wrap up the cage and bird and he would take them away with him. The heart of the monk rebelled and his lips were about to thunder no, he could not take the bird, when the thought came to him, strange if he could give up his whole life to Christ and could not give up a canary. So he bowed assent to the request of his superior. Joe, you and I and the rest of us hate to give up our little canaries. With some of us it is money, ambition, hate, bitterness or passion, but we hate to give the canary up."

"What did you say five thousand lines in the Pilot cost?" asked Mr. Donovan softly. Joe Donovan was a very good man. He was kind, sweet, loveable and very charitable.

Then came the Nash advertising through the good offices of Arthur Winn. He fought in France and found his buddy from Dakota was an exiled Jesuit priest who had come back to fight for his country. The Chevrolet and the Dodge and the Oldsmobile and the Buick and Cadillac all came in from time to time to get acquainted with Pilot readers.

There are about thirty-five accounts on my list and they include men of many nationalities. One of my most intimate friends is the most brilliant newspaper man that it has ever been my good fortune to meet. He is not of my faith nor is he a churchgoer, and yet he is a very kindly man and I know he is a very religious man. Every man who gives me any business I remember not only at Christmas and Easter with a good wish suitable for the season, but I never miss a day in recommending them to Him who made all things. This is a command of the church that we must pray for our benefactors and ask that they be rewarded a hundred fold. I have many friends whom I love and I don't meet in a business way, and for these I especially ask favors from the Giver of Gifts.

A long time ago I made a compact with four religious sisters, a Dominican sister, one who wears the garb of the Sisters of Notre Dame, another who is a Sister of St. Joseph, and the fourth a Franciscan. These I call my four horsemen, for they have pledged themselves to pray for me every day and I for them. I have many friends among the Catholic clergymen. I found the other day that more than thirty-five of these men who have consecrated their lives to God have visited Mary and me in the little house where we live in Newton. From each of them I have learned something of value. Some great truths from the gospel or from the epistles. While I have read them myself many times, the light that they shed on them brought out their true meaning to my profit.

During all the years of my manhood while I have played a lot and have had many of the joys of life, I have always found time for the reading of good books. I have read the best in literature by many of the best writers of the world. I have seen many of the great plays and the great actors of my time. I have read the works of many of the great poets of all nations, so there have come to me many of the beautiful things of life.

My favorite author is Cardinal Newman and close seconds are Father O'Farrell, author of "Lectures of a Certain Professor," and Canon Sheehan, a great Irishman, author of many works of fiction and "Under the Cedars and The Stars."

Some time ago it was my good fortune to spend a

day with a great bishop. He, Father George and myself made a call at a great house where the mistress was a Catholic but the husband was without the faith. I suspect the purpose of this visit was to bring the good man into the church so that he and the wife could be really one. The bishop spent some time with the host, and on the way home Father George looked at him inquiringly. The bishop said, "He tells me he never read a book; my God, what can you do with a man who never read a book."

The depression which began in 1929 affected advertising revenues like every other line of business. Every year to the present year usually showed losses.

The Pilot was no exception, but felt loss of revenue probably a little more keenly than the big publications. Here in Boston the daily papers cut salaries, some three times, some twice; some did not cut any employee getting under twenty-five dollars a week. One daily, the Post, while suffering a very heavy loss in advertising revenues, did not cut a single salary or let an employee go. If they died, their places were, except in exceptional cases, unfilled. There may be other cases like the Post, but they have not come to my attention.

Nearly all employers were forced to make reductions in salaries, but many of those who were not forced to do so were glad to do it. In many cases this line of conduct was adopted by the rich, and the maid and the cooks and the gardeners were reduced in salaries. But there were some who never made a reduction in the years of hard time; but they did all that was possible to help those who were in need.

The Pilot made no reduction in salaries, but as I was a commission man there was an automatic reduction in my check. I worked harder, but, like everyone else, I could not get the business. I knew when the depression set in that it would last a period of years until men and women got back to work. The day I was sixty-six I got a part-time contract to sell insurance with the Equitable Life Assurance Society of the United States. As my contract with the Pilot was for part-time, this filled in nicely.

This is a great company, and fine body of helpful men and officers do a great business. I have sold 100 people Insurance or Annuities. The total amount is not a great deal, about $350,000 for the four years I have worked for them. I have earned about $6,000, which, with my Pilot checks, have kept the wheels going around. Then in addition I have made many new friends. There is never a time when there is not someone to see and discuss business with.

I would advise any high-grade young man to make Insurance his life work. There are usually renewals on his premiums for a number of years that will sweeten his income, and it is a business he can carry on to an advanced age. As long as you can walk and talk you can earn a living in the Insurance business. Every time you sell a policy you have done a good deed; either you will get the blessings of some beneficiary or it will be the thanks of some old man or woman you have taught how to save for old age through Life Insurance.

I have now been working sixty-three years, seventeen years in the cotton mills of Fall River, seven years in the Fall River Herald, seven years in the Fall River Globe, two years with the Ward Baking Company of Pittsburgh, fourteen years with Julius Mathews, Special Agency, ten years with the John Donnelly Company, Outdoor Advertising, seventeen years with the Pilot Publishing Company, and four years with the Equitable life Assurance Society. This, of course, covers more than the sixty-two years, for at some times I have held as many as five jobs at one time. In all I have worked for twenty-five different men, most of them pretty good scouts. Mary is still with me, and as sweet as ever. She keeps step with me, and marches bravely on. When she reaches the end of the journey and meets the Master, her hands will be filled with good deeds. She has just completed twenty-five years as First Prefect of the Sodality of our Lady. I am in good health, good courage, and have life's every promise for a pleasant old age. One of the great doctors of the Church teaches that a well spent day gives a pleasant evening.

I have never visited Ireland in all those years. But I have often been there in my dreams. Yes, I love it, for it is my native land, and when my ship comes in maybe I will have enough money to make the visit to the scenes of my childhood. But if not it may be that my soul will go through Ireland on its way to Heaven. America has been good to me. It is not perfect, but it is the greatest country in the world.

Mary has a garden and I spend in the summer much of my time there. The crocuses and tulips come up in March, then each month brings its flowers to gladden the heart of men until late October or early November the chrysanthemums come in their splendor. I find this running all through life, some men mature in crocus or tulip time and others later, while there are some who in the November of life come to maturity. So I hope that when my November comes I will have a clearer vision of things, more charity, greater kindliness toward my fellow men. I find that those who love their fellow men find more peace and happiness than those who do not.

What the future holds for me I do not know, but I

know that God will take care of me as he has until now. If I have my wish I will express it in the words of a gifted woman—

>"Jesu:
>O never let me find
>Myself too proud for human kind,
>Let me work my whole life through
>Nor find a task too light to do,
>And when I die, let me not be
>Afraid to face eternity
>But with the setting of the sun
>Hear thy gentle voice 'Well done,'
>   Jesu."

A LETTER TO PAPE

A Message to Employers and Employees Sent to William J. Pape, Publisher, Waterbury Republican, Waterbury, Connecticut

My Dear Mr. Pape:

This acknowledges the invitation sent to me a few days ago to attend a reception and banquet of the staff of the *Waterbury Republican.*

It would have been acknowledged sooner, but I delayed it, hoping to couple with the acknowledgement an acceptance to be present and address your employees at the banquet which you are tendering them. My acceptance I now find will be impossible, so I take this means of conveying my regrets.

As you know, my business as an advertising man brings me into the offices of many daily newspapers, and my training as a newspaper man has led me to observe men as I go. I have as a result certain mental prints on relations between employees and employers which may be valuable to you. These prints are the mature reflections of one who has studied business relations from the standpoint of the employer and also from that of the employee. Having looked at both sides, perhaps the ideas of one who has been carried to all parts of the country by the business he follows may interest you.

I like this "get-together" spirit which is shown for the sixth time by the members of your staff. A great deal of good must come from it. It will bring them closer together, and I believe, bring them closer to you, which is one of the great things to be desired.

Usually at staff banquets such as yours the spirit of the addresses given is to direct aright the rank and file of the employees, telling them to be loyal, to be attentive, to be faithful to their employer's interest, but seldom a word to him who usually needs it the most—the employer. Were I present, I think the best service I could render you would be to reverse the order of things somewhat. The great responsibility for the well being of the staff—which in this sense means all of your employees—rests on you, the master mind of the *Waterbury Republican.*

Wherefore, while I will render some advice suitable to employees, the employers, or any man possessing authority over others may well heed what I address to yourself as regards the men who work for you:

Any employee who does his duty, does it through the day as faithfully as though his employer was at his elbow, has nothing to fear in this life and probably not in the next. But to do this is not as easy as it seems; mere willingness is not sufficient. To be able to do a day's work well necessitates right living; the observance of moral and physical laws. There is more to this than many appreciate. A breach in nature's laws sometimes seem to have no evil consequences, but it is as immutable as the laws of physics that there can be no action without reaction.

The only difference to my mind is that the reaction or evil consequences are delayed sometimes. But a usurer's interest is extorted and ultimately payment must be made. A night's dissipation may not bring on a morning headache, but some time Nature will demand a penalty. A wrong deed may show a momentary profit, but pain inevitably follows. An evil suggestion may bring pleasure for the moment without seeming harm, but like the seed of the worm deposited on the apple blossom, the evil consequences will bore through the good fruit to your sorrow.

Happily, the reverse is true; a good deed done today without any reward will surely some day bring back reward manifold. The good suggestion that is given to men in time of temptation is engraven on our own hearts to direct us in times of trouble. The prayers we lisped at our mother's knee work for our salvation throughout our lives much like the circle made by the pebble dropped into the water, each circle becoming wider, and wider, and wider, until it passes our understanding.

To your people I finally would say that the best illustration to portray what they should do can be taken from an instance in the life of a Connecticut man, Davenport, who was presiding officer of the assembly nearly two hundred years ago.

It seems the day grew dark toward noon without apparent cause, one of the phenomena of nature, and the darker it grew, the more frightened became the members of the assembly. Everything pointed to the fact that the last day had come. All seemed to believe it so. Some cursed, many dropped on their knees and prayed, while others in abject terror listened to the trumpet call that was to summon all to final judgment, Davenport, standing erect, conscious of having through life done the best that was within him, pounded with his gavel for order, then thundered forth, "Bring in the candles and let us do our work. If this is the last day, when God comes let Him find us doing our duty."

It is well, then, for those who wish to do their duty, to their own self be true; to have clean bodies that they may be well able to bear the heat and burden of the day; to have clean minds, that they may see clearly the things of life and that they have clean hearts that they, like Davenport, fear not the trumpet call.

And now let us consider yourself. You have been placed in a position of great responsibility as head of the *Waterbury Republican* family. I have known, respected and esteemed you for many years, and I believe that you are a big man in the meaning that a man is big in his sympathies and small in his selfishness. You will appreciate that it is a desire for your welfare and the welfare of the *Republican* that leads me to write you from my heart, as I am doing in this letter.

I find that when the employer is respected there is a far greater service rendered by the employees than when he is only feared; when he is loved the heart and brain of the employees unite in pushing things that are to his best interests; when he is disliked, the effect on the work is much the same as the effects of fear and anger on the digestion.

I have said you have great responsibilities, and in the final summing up great things will be expected of you, as great opportunities were given you. You will be asked what you have done with the talents that were given you.

I know that you have higher ideals than the establishing of a great money-making newspaper; that you will not mark your success in Waterbury by the amount of profit shown on your ledger. I know you well enough to appreciate that you comprehend what the meaning of life is and that there are "results" that are never shown in the till, yet bring a solace and joy to the heart that money cannot bring.

Some time ago there was an editorial in the *Republican* to boys about the hours they should keep, the companions they should associate with, how they should employ their leisure and the respect they should give their mother. Such an editorial could only be penned by one who desired good to his fellow men, and the seed that was sowed in that editorial must have brought forth good fruit.

I feel that as publisher of a great daily newspaper you have at heart the welfare of your city and will do what you can to fight for its best interests; you will encourage all movements for the good of Waterbury and you will attack all things that mean evil to your fair city.

I appreciate that you feel that you are not only making a paper, but that you are making a life which inspires me to write you as I do.

It is possible for an employer to hang up a sign in his place of business directing the employees to love, honor and respect him, but were he to believe his order would be complied with, he would be entitled to a nice padded room in an asylum.

You can command the body of man, but the mind and soul are free, and these three attributes of the soul above mentioned must be won, and can only be won by the deserving. It follows, then that you must have in you the positive qualities of mind and soul which attract this trinity from those who are in daily contact with you, much as the flowers open their petals to the warm rays of the morning sun, and close again as he bids them good night and sinks below the western hills.

What is there in an employer that these three attributes demand before they will shower their graces on him? Frankly, I can only tell you in a general way some things that have come under my observation from a service of more than forty years. I find these positive qualities are possessed by the genial man—one who has warmth and love for his fellow men. I notice how all the beautiful flowers of the universe live and thrive in warm places. It seems to me in the heart of a genial man there is warmth for the flowers of human affections to grow.

An employer must have a sense of fairness. He has, in his relations with his employees, a giant's strength, and without a sense of fairness he has the bruteness of the savage. He holds the scales and reads the measure, and if he takes advantage of the employees, he kills affections and the qualities that flow therefrom. He may have spent years in training his man, but by an act of injustice he divorces the latter more surely than any decree of human court could do. This act of injustice will have its reaction when he least expects it, and probably when he is least able to meet it.

The fair employer takes all employees at their true worth, as nearly as he can appreciate it. He is free from all traits of prejudice which come from race, religion or social standing. The man big enough in his sympathies to look upon all men as brothers never favors one of "our own kind" at the expense of others. When a fear that such is the case creeps into the hearts of those who strive for advancement through merit they are very likely to look somewhere else for reward. Meanwhile their services have not the value that they had.

The good employer is charitable—not only in the sense of giving to the needy, but in overlooking the frailties of human nature which are ever coming under his observation. A kindly talk, a little moral help, and sometimes a little financial help may stop a man from going to hell any day, while bitter reproaches only grease the way to make him slide down more quickly. One of the most successful employers I ever knew told me that his great secret was never to see too much of the little failings that seem common in human nature men are heir to.

It seems to me that the rank and file have been given greater intuition than those who occupy higher places such as you who depend on the intellect for reaching conclusions. The employer who has taken some dislike to an employee and nourishes this dislike, though giving no expression to it, thinks it is hidden safe in his heart, yet he betrays it daily by his bearing and even the tone of his voice seems to shriek it to that employee. We learn from this that it is better to "talk it over" with the employee and have a thorough understanding, thus preventing what will otherwise in the long run end in a breach that cannot be healed.

These thoughts of mine will reach you on Washington's Birthday. He won the love and respect and the confidence of the people of this country by his greatness of mind and soul. Let us hope that each of us in our way and in our own little world imitate his good qualities as closely as we can.

Very truly yours,
DAVID S. LAWLOR

Mr. William J. Pape
Waterbury, Ct.

MY MASTER'S HOUSE

An Address Given to the Armour Oval Label Club of Boston

Your name, the Oval Club, brings to my mind one of the most beautiful pictures in history. Sacred Scripture tells that when the angel of the Lord warned St. Joseph and directed him to take Mary and Jesus into Egypt, their flight was preceded by an oval of light.

Many of the great artists of the world have tried to reproduce this oval in their Madonnas, but only Raphael succeeded. It is shown in his wonderful Madonna Gonzaga painted for the grandmother of St. Aloysius, and was found in his studio at his death.

Rev. Father Glodt, a great art critic, tells me that this is a masterpiece and one of the great paintings of the world. He is an authority on art, having spent fourteen years in the Louvre at Paris.

This great painting, the original, is here in Boston in the Duffee studio on Boylston Street. I would suggest that each of you see it, as its great beauty will leave its impression on you forever.

This is an age of specialization. A man is taught specially to do one thing or to sell one thing; and usually, where chance first starts a man, he follows until the bell tolls. There are notable exceptions, however—men who will not stay put. These are the men who recognize that while they are salesmen, mechanics, or laborers, they are above all else—men. Every one of us should realize this great truth, that while there is a universal need for special skill, for a man to have a special education in one direction, he is more than a salesman, a plumber, a mechanic or an advertising man—that before and after everything else, he is a man.

This is to be a man to man talk between you and me. These are serious times, and a little serious talk on the things that are in life worth while may be of advantage to some of you. I say some of you because I have in mind the gospel that tells of the sower that went out to sow his seed:

> "And as he sowed, some fell by the wayside, and it was trodden down and the birds of the air ate it up. And some fell on the rock, and as soon as it had sprung up it withered away because it had no moisture. And some fell among thorns, and the thorns, growing up with it, choked it. And some fell on good ground, and sprang up and yielded fruit one hundred fold."

Wonderful are the works of man. He has circumnavigated the globe; traced great rivers to their sources; climbed the highest mountains; discovered the two great poles; measured the distance to the stars and weighed the sun, but no man has yet lived who has been able to circumnavigate man. Today man is almost as much of a mystery as he was in the beginning, and he is as little understood. It would seem as though the work of the infinite mind was beyond the understanding of the finite mind.

Your sales manager gave me a half hour to talk to you on the mind of man; on the ethical side of life. I refused on the ground that the subject was so great, so comprehensive, that it appalled me, but he insisted and said that if I were only to put in the foundation or even briefly to sketch some of the things that a man ought to know to help him to be a greater man, my work would be appreciated.

Much has been said in a half hour. Thirty of the world's greatest speeches which have come down in history as the greatest efforts of orators, more than half of them, were spoken in fifteen minutes. Lincoln's great speech at Gettysburg, a speech that will go down the ages, was delivered in less than five minutes. Much then may be said in a half hour. If in that time I can help you to be abler men, stronger men, better men; if I can show you how to overcome many of the little things that are doing you harm and show you how to strengthen the many things that will do you good; if I can point out to you and warn you of the road that will lead to trouble and pain, and set you on the road that will lead to health and happiness and peace of mind, then I will feel that I have been well rewarded for the time I have given you.

Let me know you better. You are salesmen for the Armour Company. You give your company the best that is in you, say eight hours of every day. Well and good! Where do you live? What kind of a house do you live in and where is it situated? How is your home furnished, and what kind of a man is the master of the house you live in? Is your home on an alley, or on an avenue? Is it a cottage, neat and attractive on a country road, or is it some abode going to wrack and ruin in some evil neighborhood?

I hope it is a mansion on a broad avenue, the house surrounded by noble specimens of the forest; flowers and plants here and there that show the love for the beautiful by the owner.

In such a house I expect to find the rooms large and

high studded, the furnishings rich and in good taste, beautiful paintings on the wall, a library well stocked with the choicest literature of the ages.

I expect to find an atmosphere of rest, of comfort and of peace; and when the master comes to find a man who has the air of a master, with mind and bearing denoting to the manner born. There is will on the throne directing events, and it is will correlated to pure thoughts and high ideals.

Any of you may have such a home as I have described. The body is the home; the broad avenue is the atmosphere the thoughts occupy; the magnificent trees are the good resolutions that have been made and kept; the flowers are the beautiful deeds done in life; the dwelling place with its great rooms is the broadness of vision; the oil paintings are the beautiful thoughts that come with right living, and the well stocked library is the mind that has been refreshed by contact with the great minds of the centuries. Surely such a home is desirable, and is worth any effort that it may cost.

Your body is the jewel case in which reside the heart, the mind and the soul. You have been taught from infancy the care of this body. It is well worth your care. Nature demands it be cared for, and punishes severely any injury to it. Respect your bodies, for usually with a clean body goes a clean mind. I do not mean the soil that comes from honest toil, but the stain that comes from excesses and debaucheries that soil not only the body, but which leave their impress on the mind and the soul.

I might liken the body to a ship; the mind to the rudder of the ship that gives it direction; the will the captain, who directs the course; the conscience, the charts which show the channels through which the ship may sail in safety, and mark the rocks and the shoals upon which there is danger of wreck and destruction. Let us very briefly examine the growth of this mentality which gives us character.

"Our body began as a speck of vitalized protoplasm that developed in dark and in secret," says Dr. Openheim. "It came into the world with a cry of pain, and then began the struggle of life; and with the growth of the body came the growth of the mind, less easily seen, but still developing from time to time.

"This development of the body continues for a certain length of time until maturity arrives, the time for active work. Then growth ceases, and an even level of strength is kept up until middle life, when the physical resources begin to decline. Slowly weakness creeps on, and each year man finds himself less able to withstand the wear and tear. Thus old age arrives, and with a cry of pain and a sigh of resignation we go to our reward.

"The mind during all this time does not keep up an even pace in its progression; it differs from the body in being more influenced by environment than by heredity. The mind starts out as a fluid whose final crystalized form is the forces that have been working upon it, good and bad, wise and unwise. These forces are influencing it each day, each hour. There is the same struggle between influences as there is between animals in the primeval lands or trees in the forests. Those that are naturally strong and have most favorable environments grow briskly, and those that are less favorably placed die out. We are totally unconscious of being a battlefield where one sort of victory or another must be decided."

As those things which so closely influence our lives are vital to us, let us pause and examine them.

Heredity is not of our choice. Our fathers and mothers are thrust upon us, as we have no choice in the selection. Probably we could not make as good a choice as Nature did for us. This, strange to say, has but very little influence on our lives; at least, so the best authorities declare. The great moulder of our character is environment, and the greatest of environments is the home circle, the outlook of life that is given to us by our fathers and mothers, and our home surroundings.

Environment is more than the family circle, more than the neighborhood in which we live. Environment means association; the chums we associate with; the books we read, the schools we attend; the pictures we see, and the thousand things that come into our daily life. It is said that the mind takes fifty thousand impressions a day. See to it, we should, that these pictures are clean, inspiring and elevating, if we would have a mind that will guide us right, a mind that will be a source of joy and pleasure to us, and to all whom we come in contact with, a mind that will give a fragrance to our whole being. Such a mind is a jewel beyond price.

How is such a mind to be attained? By discipline, by drill, mental drill much like bodily drill. You have seen many of the boys from your neighborhood taken in the draft, round shouldered, narrow chested boys. They were sent to Camp Devens or some other cantonment; and you have seen them some months afterwards, their carriage erect, their chests broad and their shoulders square. Physically they were better men. What made this change? Drill, drill, everlasting drill.

The mind may be drilled much the same way, but there must be the will to do it, and that will must come from within. It cannot come from without. An internal treatment or influence must stir it into life. We must keep it awakened by constant exercise, and such exercise will win health and vigor for our will. When we have done this, we will recognize within us a new force capable of achieving much. Usually that means that we have a new possession in our mind from which to work and develop aright and draw forth untold riches.

Every good, healthy concern from time to time takes stock, and every good, healthy man should take stock of himself every so often to find out his weaknesses and correct them before they have become a habit; to see what his virtues are that he may encourage them to even a greater growth. The value of these introspections is worth while. A good physician will never prescribe unless he knows what is the ailment. There is first the diagnosis and then the treatment. Let us find out in what we are deficient; then bring up our forces and supply the deficiency.

Do you swear? Stop it. Once a salesmanager told me that he would give anything to give up the evil. For twenty years he had been swearing many times a day. I asked him why he did not stop it, and he said that he could not. I told him that he would cure himself if only he would follow my advice: first make the resolution to stop swearing; second write a memo each days as follows: "I promise that I will not swear today, and if by chance I do swear, I will immediately write out this same promise." He did so. He told me that the method was wonderful, as the second day he was cured.

Have you a bad temper? Then cure it. Professor James says that the way to cure a bad temper is to deny it expression, and then it dies a natural death.

A strong passion may be subdued by refusing it freedom of action. Habits are made and grow stronger by repeated acts; they are unmade, or made weaker by constant denial. Men who have gone deeply into the science of the mind say that the set teeth and the clinched hands are not symptoms but the cause of anger. When you are tempted to be angry, instead of letting the corners of the mouth droop, just smile, and the sunshine from that smile will dissolve the angry feeling just as ice dissolves from the warmth of the sun.

As to the habit of drink, I will quote from Dr. E. Boyd Barrett: "Suffice it to say that it poisons the blood, and that the blood is no longer able to nourish the nerve tissues. As a consequence the healthiness and capacity for work of the inebriate diminish. Just as vigorous health, full pure-blooded fitness, is the optimal condition for making volitional effort, so the nervous debility consequent on intoxication is the worst possible condition for such effort making. He may think and his friends may think that he could, if he tried, give up drink, but when things have gone so far it is all but impossible. Only extraordinary circumstances and the help of God's grace can then save him.

"It is in presence of such considerations that Professor James writes as follows: 'The hell to be endured hereafter, of which theology tells, is no worse than the hell we make for ourselves in this world by habitually fashioning our characters in the wrong way. Could the young but realize how soon they will become mere walking bundles of habits, they would give more heed to their conduct while it is in the plastic state. We are spinning our own fates, good or evil, and never to be undone.'"

I knew a man once who had gone into the gutter

through drink. He lost his job, his friends, and his money. He came back, and he has stayed back all this time—and that was more than twenty-five years ago.

"How did you do it, Ned?" I asked. "I resolved to cut it out; then made a vow that I would not only cut it out, but would cut out every place where it was sold, and cut out of my life every man who drinks liquor." That was his answer.

This man, by the grace of God, used the same method as is advised by the church after the accumulated wisdom of nearly 2,000 years—shun the occasion, shun the place and shun the companionship.

The sick wills have been divided into eight classes, all amenable to treatment. There are the hesitating, the impulsive, the inactive, the "I can't," the overactive and the emotional will, and the over-practical and the indefinite will.

If you are impatient and hot headed, and go off at half-cock try Dr. Barrett's treatment for such a case. Each action ought to be done once a day for ten days and occupy ten minutes in the doing; and, at the end of each exercise, one is to write each day his introspection—

1. To replace in a box very slowly and deliberately one hundred matches.
2. To write out very slowly and carefully the words, "I will train my will."
3. To turn over very slowly and deliberately all the leaves in a book, about 200 pages.
4. To watch the movements of the second hand of a clock or watch, and pronounce some word slowly at the completion of each minute.

There are many other exercises, each of them drilling the will much as the drill sergeant makes over the bodies of our boys in army cantonments.

The great object of self-discipline is, in reality, to brace the human will for the strengthening of the moral life.

The education of the will must not be left to fate, nor can it be left to others. It must be carried out by ourselves. It must be carried out in accordance with the knowledge we can ourself acquire of our individual self. Study, introspection, and self-discipline must then go hand in hand. Effort and patience are the price to be paid. There is no mystery, there is no short cut; the goal to each is self-mastery, personal power and force of character. The way is long, the way is hard, but the goal is worth the winning.

There are five rules, as given by Dr. Barrett, that we ought all make a part of our lives:—

1. We must make our nervous system our ally instead of our enemy.

2. In the acquisition of a new habit or the leaving off of an old one, we must take care to launch ourselves with as strong and decided initiative as possible.

3. Never suffer an exception to occur until the new habit is securely rooted in life.

4. Seize the very first possible opportunity to act on every resolution you make and on every emotional prompting you may experience in the direction of the habits you aspire to gain.

5. Keep the faculties of effort alive in you by a little gratuitous exercise every day.

Here then is given you a plan to build, decorate and furnish your master's house. You can build it on any scale and make it as beautiful as your heart desires.

In it you can have many of the treasures of the world that will always be a source of joy to you. You are the master of your own fate. You can build as you desire, but you must pay the price in work. You cannot pay for it with a smile or by check.

Work, work, work! It was decreed that we must win by the sweat of our brow, but oh, the joy that comes from honest, well directed effort! Nature royally treats her children who rigidly observe her laws. To them she gives health, strength and power. Just a few words more and I am done. Our place here has been called "the garden of life," and it has been said by an unknown poet:—

>Beautiful thoughts make beautiful lives,
>   For every word and deed
>Lies in the thought that prompted it
>   As the flower lies in the seed.
>
>Back of each action lay the thought
>   We nourished until it grew
>Into a work, or into a deed,
>   That marked our life work through.
>
>Gracious words and kindly ways,
>   Deeds that are high and true;
>Slanderous words and hasty words
>   And deeds we bitterly rue.
>
>The garden of life, it beareth well;
>   It will repay our care,
>But the blossom must always and ever be
>   Like the seed we're planting there.

THE GREATEST MOTHER IN THE WORLD

*An Address Given to Winthrop Council,
Knights of Columbus*

"You have knelt at the table of Our Lord and He has given you of His Body and Blood, and restored the innocence of your childhood. He has made you little children again, which is necessary for anyone to enter the kingdom of heaven.

"Now, we are all together. What will we do? It is too early for story telling, for you know that the children's hour is 'between the dark and the daylight.' A speech? Who cares for a long and serious talk so early in the morning? I have it. We will take a ramble out on the highways of life.

> "They say that life is a highway
>   And its milestones are the years.
> And now and then there's a toll gate
>   Where you buy your way with tears.
> It is a rough road and a steep road
>   And it is stretched broad and far
> But at last it leads to a golden town
>   Where golden houses are."

"Here we are, outdoors, the greatest thing in this world that God has made. See the people passing by, sage and singer, saint and sinner, all in search of happiness. Here are men of every degree, the high and the low, the rich and the poor. Some riding but many afoot. Some smiling, some crying, a few praying, but all hurrying along to the golden town where the golden houses are.

"Let us behold the wonders of God all about us. Far out are the mountains and then the valley. And the sun, symbolic of the love of Christ, warms all Mother Earth and gives us life. Here is the grass and the flowers and the trees and the birds. Let us for an instant give glory to God for the wonders He has created for us.

"See this old Abbé on foot and alone. I know his story. He told me that for fifty years he was a curé in a little French hamlet, fell ill and thought he awoke in the arms of his Creator. God asked him how he liked the beautiful world He had made for him and for other men. A feeling of sadness came over the Abbé and he thought if he had life to live over again he would see more of this beautiful world. Recovering he had started out on his journey and had traversed this country on foot from ocean to ocean. Let us see as much of his beautiful world as we can.

"There is the home of the Little Sisters of the Poor. In that house they have many old men and women who are depending on them for food and shelter. These good Sisters have nothing and beg, not for themselves, but for God's poor.

In these two houses they have about 600 men and women. The youngest taken is 65 years of age. No questions of faith is asked. If they are homeless and penniless that is sufficient.

"A good priest who was their chaplain for many years told me wonderful stories of the faith of these good Sisters. Their patron saint is St. Joseph and no matter what they want they appeal to St. Joseph. Many a day in winter one of the Sisters would go to the Superior and say, 'Mother, there is not a loaf of bread in the house, just a crust. Where will we get the bread for the men and women who will be looking for their meal soon? We cannot go out because the snow is three feet deep.' And the Mother would say, 'Well, put a crust on St. Joseph's altar, and tell St. Joseph we want bread.' In a little while a messenger would arrive and say, "Mother, I am from So and So's bakery. On account of the storm we cannot get our wagons out and we have about four or five hundred loaves of bread here that we cannot use. Would you want us to send them over to you?" Or it might be that it was coal they needed and the last few grains would be in the bin and the weather would be cold, so a lump of coal would be put on St. Joseph's altar and some time during the day some man or woman would come in and ask: 'Mother, how are you getting along this cold weather? How would you like a half a dozen tons of coal?' Then the coal would come. This good priest, God bless him, was sent out to found a parish, one of the smallest parishes in the diocese, only three hundred families. He got there Friday afternoon and there was not a place for him to say mass, not even a vacant house. He told the good Sisters and they appealed to St. Joseph. Next morning he found a man who had built a big apartment house and who had foolishly built a big garage behind it that was big enough to hold two or three times the number of automobiles then in the whole district. God works in a mysterious way. Only He and St. Joseph maybe knew why the garage was built, but it housed the good priest and his congregation for four or five years. And now there is a beautiful church on the hill that is said to be the gem of the diocese.

"There is a bit of land adjoining this church that

the pastor wanted but he did not have the money to pay for it nor did he know where he was going to get it. So one day he and his beloved curate dug a tiny hole on that land and they buried in there a little image of St. Joseph and told him to get that land. Well, the church owns the land now and there is a $30,000 School house on it.

"But we must be on our way. Here come two Sisters of Charity, on some errand of mercy, no doubt. Salute them, for here is royalty. They, and all who wear their garb, are ladies in waiting to Her Majesty, Mary, Queen of Heaven and Earth. How much do we owe these good Sisters for their good work and unceasing prayers ever ascending to the Mother of God to speak a good word for us to Her Divine Son.

"Mother of Christ, Mother of Christ
He was all and all to thee,
In the wind-swept cave, in the
Nazareth home, in the hamlet of Galilee
Mother of Christ, Mother of Christ
He will not say nay to thee
When He turns His face to thy sweet embrace
Then Mother, speak of me."

Some years ago, talking with the Mother of the House of the Good Shepherd, I said: "Mother, you are doing a great work." And she said: "All the religious orders in the Catholic Church are doing a great and good work." It is so. If we favor one more than another it is because we get a more intimate view of it. We get closer to it and if we get closer to the others we would love them just as much.

"This great massive building on the right is St. Elizabeth's, a monument of Catholic charities. What wonderful work there is being done here every day. Let us say a prayer for those in pain each time we pass and ask the Almighty to remember us in our last agony.

"The Sisters tell me that there have been many conversions of Protestant doctors who have given of their skill to Catholic patients. The fervent 'God bless you, doctor,' from grateful men and women has brought many doctors close to the Divine Master.

"St. Elizabeth's, by the way, draws no line on creed or nativity. This hospital ministers alike to all of God's children in sickness.

"These two priests coming out of St. Elizabeth's are the editor of the Pilot and his editorial assistant. I hope you all read the Pilot and that those who are dear to you read it, for the Pilot is the defender of the Church. It brings to you light in all matters of religion and solace to you in your afflictions. There are 200,000 Catholic homes in this archdiocese and the Pilot goes into one in four homes, or a trifle over 50,000 families. It should be in every Catholic home. What a wonderful power the Pilot would be for the Church if it was received into every Catholic home!

"The Pilot is your paper. It is published solely for your spiritual and material good. It is hardly enough to subscribe for it and read it. It costs more to produce the Pilot than you pay for it. The two dollars a year subscription does not cover the cost of publication. Merchants must get returns for their advertising or they cease to advertise. If you gentlemen and your wives and sisters will mention the Pilot when purchasing goods it will help a great deal. I believe as an advertising man that advertising in the Pilot, like good seed planted in good ground, will bring a good reward to those who plant it. The readers of the Pilot purchase goods for 350,000 people, for I believe that our statistics show in the church seven to a family, though the government only shows an average of 4.5 for the country. I have only touched on the business side, but from the moral and intellectual side those who read the Pilot gain largely in the good things of life. Many of you read the splendid editorials in the Pilot. They are a treat like all enjoyable, safe sane literature.

"I hope you read the Looker-on column in the Pilot. They who read it week after week are given a store of knowledge that otherwise would never come to them. These articles from week to week cling to the memory and bring pleasant memories as we travel along the highways of life.

"You might with profit read the Book Reviews of the Pilot. It points out the good books to read. Books are like men and women. You would like to have good men and women visit you, why not have good books come into your home. There are men and women whom you would not allow to cross the threshold of your home, but sometimes they are allowed in book form, and they bring their evil message, and they leave a curse behind them. The columns in the Pilot devoted to the propagation of the faith, letters from the missionaries and news of various orders who carrying message of Church into heathen fields is vivid and of great interest.

Then there is the page from the Charitable Bureau. This bureau has more than three hundred boys in its care and would like some help. Its message is appealing for "God whispers in your ear when tempted to do a good deed."

The beautiful poems and sonnets of Jesus and his Mother that appear every week in the Pilot will repay anyone a hundredfold for the subscription price of the Pilot.

There are I believe sixty catholic magazines published. In every one of them you will find some thought which will repay you for the price. Let me suggest a few though all are worthy: The Sign, America, Truth, Extension, and the Catholic World.

"Are you, boys, members of the Holy Name and kindred sodalities? Do you help your pastor in his financial activities, his field days, and various church events that mean so much to him? Do you belong to the church debt society and do you give generously to the collections? These are your obligations and you must meet them.

"Here we are at the Monastery of St. Gabriel. This is Father George, the director of retreats. You have had fifty of these boys on retreat, Father, and by and by the others will come. We thought you would let us in the beautiful Monastery Chapel, Father, that we might say a little prayer for ourselves and those we love.

"Here is the chapel. Is it not beautiful? The priest and students kneel in those stalls around the chapel, and we occupy them in the retreats. Let me just sketch what one of these retreats is like. The men come on a Friday evening, about 25 in number, and they stay till Monday morning. There are about eight conferences in the little chapel, just man to man talks (about sin and its dangers to the soul). You leave the world behind so here is the time for meditation and prayer. There is an opportunity for confession and Communion, and Monday morning while the city sleeps you assist at the Mass and Benediction. Then you get the Papal Blessing, breakfast and with a clean heart you face the world.

"Father Garache gives a beautiful simile which shows the necessity for retreats. He compares the soul to a clear body of water which reflects the beauty of the heavens, but when that water is no longer clear it fails to show the reflection. Sin, he says, so dims the soul that it no longer can reflect the purity and clearness of God so it is necessary to keep the soul pure and clean.

"Let us go out on the cloister and see the wonderful view. Permit me to point out to you some of the various Catholic houses of activities. Here is one of the spiritual fortresses that protect our city. From this spot and similar religious houses that surround our beloved city and also that surround our beloved country there is ascending every hour of the day petitions to the Most High to spare our people.

Look to the North, there in Cambridge is the Holy Ghost Hospital for cancer patients. There the good Grey Nuns devote their lives to those who are incurable. Turn to the East and you can see St. Mary's Infant Asylum. Here babies that come from heaven are welcomed, and their mothers nursed back to health for the love of Him who forgave the Sinner.

In the heart of the city below in the home for destitute children in care of the Sisters of Charity, and a little nearer this way you can see the House of the Good Shepherd where unfortunate girls get good advice, affection and are put back on the right road.

Around you in this diocese are more than two hundred and fifty catholic churches, a hundred or more parochial schools that instruct more than eighty thousand of our children; there are many convents for the teaching staff of these schools are the good sisters of St. Joseph, or the ever smiling Sisters of Notre Dame and twenty-five other orders of teaching Sisters and six orders of men teachers. They give their all. What do we give?

Great is the faith that built these great buildings, the money comes from the labor of God-fearing men and women of limited means. Somewhere I read this beautiful thought:

"Imagine a rose that would say to itself—'I cannot afford to give away all my beauty and sweetness. I must keep it for myself. I will roll up my petals and withhold my fragrance,'—but behold, the moment the rose tries to store up its colors and treasures of fragrance to withhold them from others, they vanish. The colors and fragrance do not exist in the unopened bud.

It is only when the rose begins to open itself to give out its sweetness, its life to others, that its beauty and sweetness are developed. He who refuses to give himself for others, who closes the petals of his charity and withholds the fragrance of his sympathy and love finds that he loses the very thing he tries to keep. The springs of his manhood dry up, his fine nature becomes atrophied; he grows deaf to the cries of help from his fellow men. Tears that are never shed for other's woes sour to stinging acids in his own heart.

Refuse to open your purse and soon you cannot open your sympathy; refuse to give and you will soon cease to enjoy what you have; refuse to love and you lose the power to love and be loved. But the moment you open wider the door of your life, and like the rose send out without stint your fragrance and beauty, you let the sunshine of life into your soul."

"When the forces of evil come to attack us, it is fortresses such as this that will repulse the enemy with their prayers and petitions to Him who rules the world. From this hilltop we see St. John's Seminary, the spiritual West Point of our diocese. Caesar stamped his image and the value on his coin, so does

AN IRISH BOY IN AMERICA

God. He stamps His Image and the value on the face of each of us. Look on the faces of those who have had four years of thoughts of war, and then look at the faces of those who have had four years of thoughts of love and peace. To whom will we trust the destiny of this country? To whom will we look for succor in the hour of our need? This sword is powerless, unless the soul of him who wields it belongs to God.

But we cannot linger here any longer in this delightful spot. We must be on our way.

This beautiful group of buildings is Boston College. In this college are boys in their earliest years who have their minds imbued with the best literature and with love of Christ. Here they are taught to think correctly and associate with good men to form character. This and every Catholic educational institution is erected to the glory of God, and the love of the Lord, Jesus Christ. Give your boys a catholic education for there is safety.

That gentleman passing is a famous architect. He is not a Catholic, but is a great defender of the church and surely belongs to the soul of the church. More than twenty-five years ago he was an architect of genius, but without a client. He was discovered by a Catholic priest, who gave him his first commission to build a Gothic Church in a city of spindles and looms. This good priest wanted a beautiful church and it crowns the hill overlooking the city, but the sweet and gentle priest has gone to his Maker, preceded by his many good deeds.

The architect was asked by the government to compete for the five million dollars worth of buildings, for which the commission would be $250,000. Of course, it would mean considerable expense in getting up the plans, but the young architect threw the proposition in the waste basket because he felt he did not have a chance as it was a political job. The priest, believing in the young man's genius, told him he had a wonderful friend in his city, who was a man of great power, and he would interest this man in the architect if he would compete. To shorten the story, the architect competed with some sixty or seventy others and, lo and behold, he won the prize. Some time afterwards he took his check book to the good priest and wanted to settle with the great man whose political pull had won him the commission. Then the Father confessed that this great man was St. Anthony. Every day the priest had burned two candles at the altar and prayed to St. Anthony to find the job for his protege. As I said, the architect did not become a Catholic, but I believe that the beautiful reredos of this church was given by him as a testimonial of the power of St. Anthony.

Here we are at the cross-roads. There stands a radiant angel, who directs all travelers. He is Conscience. Stand back, boys, for here rides the warrior on his mettlesome steed. Listen! He asks for the road to fame and the angel says: "To the left, but do not go too far." Another comes in great haste. It is the statesman! What does he want? Oh, it is power he wants. "To the left," the angel says, "but don't go too far." Again another. Why, it is the financier! The road to fortune, he demands, and again the angel says, "To the left, but don't go too far." Now comes a traveler on foot, a workman with his bag of tools upon his back, a child in his arms and a woman by his side. "What road do you wish?" asks the angel. "The road to happiness." "Then take the road to the right," says the angel with a smile. "At the end of the road you will find Heaven." The woman, with the curiosity of Eve, turns and asks the angel where the other road leads and the angel answers her: "Ruin."

Fame! What is it? The most famous deed in history, one that has been told for nearly 2,000 years in every village, hamlet and city in the world; yes, even among the savage tribes, and it will be told as long as the world lasts. This story is the deed of the good Samaritan, who found his fellow man robbed and wounded and left on the highway to die. The Samaritan dressed his wounds and took him to the inn and paid for his way until he was able to be about his business. If you would be famous, imitate this great deed.

Power! What is it? Napoleon in his last days said that the three most powerful men were Alexander, Caesar and himself. Alexander, he said, died a drunkard's death, Caesar fell by the knives of his enemies, and he, Napoleon, on a barren rock in the Pacific, was ending his days. But he said: "Our power was the sword, but Christ, whose weapon was love, has triumphed and his dominion grows greater and greater year by year." It is said that the massive gates of heaven swing open to the push of the strong arm of a Trappist monk and to the gentle touch of a little child. If you would be powerful, imitate these.

Riches! What are they? There are no riches but spiritual riches, for they alone bring happiness. An old Dominican told me in boyhood that, years before, in France, a committee of Jews and Gentiles, Catholics and Protestants, Agnostics and atheists, went through France and reported unanimously that happiness was found only where the ten commandments were observed. The first four lines of today's Gospel tells you where it is found: "My Father will take up his abode with those who keep His word." If you want riches, take your lesson from the Gospel.

Let us gather flowers as we go along the highway.

"Who made you, little ones; who
Made you so lovely and so frail."

"In what garden of Eden did He behold your prototypes? Or was it from the secret of His own surpassing beauty He devised your loveliness and made you another and meeker manifestation of that undying principle that underlies every operation of His handmaid, Nature—the principle that all things round to beauty, and that, in the spiral of a vast nebula which covers half the heavens, and in the curve of a little leaf that shelters a tiny insect, order and beauty, and proportion and harmony subsist—a reflex of the Mind of the Eternal?' This beautiful thought is from Canon Sheehan.

"This great building and these fifty acres is the Working Boys' Home. Here are twelve Christian Brothers taking care of 125 little boys from ten to fifteen years of age. These children have no fathers or mothers or, at least, none to claim them. These good brothers work night and day for these little boys so that they will be warm in body and clean of mind and pure of soul. They are so far from the world that the world somehow forgets them. This home needs your help. These boys are Catholics and Protestants, for no religious lines are kept by these good Brothers. When God sends a boy to them, that is enough, they ask no questions, but do the best they can for him.

"These Brothers work from five in the morning till ten at night. The children work and study, but, of course, suitable to their years. Often a boy will ask: 'Brother Fabian, who were my father and my mother?

Why don't they come to see me?' But all the answer he can give the boy is an evasive one. For the boy's father or mother heeded not the warning of the angel at the crossroads.

"It is a good thing we came here today. The Massachusetts Catholic Women's Guild are here today. The State Regent, gave a dinner to these boys, and the Guild also gave blouses, stockings and other things. This is a yearly event with these good women. This great society, to which your sisters and wives and mothers may belong, has given to charity $7,000, but the world does not know much about it. They gave a Christmas dinner to the children of the Home for Destitute Catholic Children and they had a gift for each boy and girl in the home.

"These good women, you see, have a boy on each arm, so your help will be timely. These boys would like, it seems to me, marbles, tops, boats and 'choo-choo cars,' and playthings like what your boys like. If you give them, when you see your boy playing, a warm glow will come around your heart. The little birds and the gentle winds carry the seed from fields and forests to distant places; it may be that the seed I have sown today will grow in some heart.

"The way has been long and we are tired. Let us rest beneath these trees.

"A tree that looks at God all day
And lifts her leafy arms to pray."

"The bones of Joyce Kilmer lie in a soldier's grave in France, his soul is in Heaven, I pray. I wish I could read to you The Tree, his Blue Valentine, a beautiful poem to Our Lady, or the Hostler and the Fourth

Shepherd. The love of God and His Blessed Mother and his fellow men is shown in many of his poems, but

> "Hark! The vesper bells are ringing!
> From the dawn of the day
> Til the matin shall chime
> Shield us from danger, and
> Save us from crime."

"Our Mother, the Church, is calling her children. Mother, we are coming!

"The Catholic Church, the greatest mother in the world. She takes us in her arms as an infant, cleans us from sin and puts on our foreheads the sign of Christ. In childhood she unfolds to us the mysteries of life; in boyhood, she confirms us with a Sacrament and makes us strong and perfect Christians. She guides our steps, ever helping us to avoid pitfalls and dangers. In manhood she gives us the Sacrament of Matrimony and blesses our union that it may be fruitful and joyous. In the battle of life she is always with us, giving us solace in our sorrows. In weakness and sorrow she is ever with us, giving us comfort. In old age, or when we are summoned to appear before The Master, she gives us the Bread of Life and marks us as His own and sends us with resignation, if not joyously, into the presence of our Maker. She does not forget us after we are gone, for her prayers are ever going up to the Throne of Mercy for us.

"Yes, indeed, she is the greatest mother in the world. This month of May she devotes to the canonization of her children whose heroic virtues have won for them sainthood. She picks out the virtues most needed when she brings these virtues to the attention of the world. This month she has canonized Joan of

Arc, a French maiden whom God sent to release France from bondage; St. Gabriel, a humble Belgian youth, whose great virtue was the ardent love of Jesus crucified and by his tender compassion for His sorrowful mother; St. Margaret Mary Alicoque, whose wonderful devotion to the Sacred Heart has given her the crown of sainthood, and today, at the present time, our own great and good Cardinal is celebrating the canonization of a great Irishman, Oliver Plunkett, Archbishop of Armagh, whose love for his country and his religion led an English judge to send him to the scaffold.

"The world has its crosses and medals for valor of the body, but the Church gives crowns to these heroic souls, whose virtues may be imitated and make the world better.

"It is the hour of Benediction! The O Salutaris comes to us through the open windows of the church. It is the prayer to Him which was written by St. Thomas Aquinas, the Angelic Doctor, nearly seven hundred years ago. Jesus is on the altar. Let us prostrate ourselves before Him, petition His mercy for those dear to us who have gone before, and for those we love, that all will be well with them. Then let us each and every one of us say: 'Jesus, let us take You by the hand walk with You. Let Your way be our way, Your thoughts be our thoughts, let Your actions be our actions. Lead me and mine along life's highway, protecting us in soul and body till, in the fruitage of years, we cry to Thee like tired little children to take us in Your arms and carry us through all eternity.'

"Blessed be the name of Jesus."

THE JOURNEY OF FATHER BEPPO

An Ancient Tradition of the Church

One morning some hundreds of years ago, the good superior of the monastery of St. Dominic, which crowns one of the hills in central Europe, called Fr. Beppo and bade him prepare for a journey to begin that morning to a brother-house some 70 miles away.

The fatherly eye of the superior had noted that Fr. Beppo was not looking very well, and so he had planned this journey with the hope that the change of scene would refresh the mind, and bring vigor to the body of his comrade in Christ.

In half an hour Fr. Beppo was ready for his journey. He had knelt before his Lord in the Tabernacle, had petitioned the Blessed Mother to take him under her protection and guard him from the dangers of the road, and had bidden adieu to his fellow workers. Fr. Beppo was slowly descending the hill when the monastery bell rang for the Angelus, and as his ears got the first sound he sang aloud:

"The angel of the Lord declared unto Mary and she conceived of the Holy Ghost.

"Behold the handmaid of the Lord, be it done unto me according to Thy Word.

"The Word was made flesh and dwelt amongst us.

"Pray for us holy mother of God that we may be made worthy of the promises of Christ.

AN IRISH BOY IN AMERICA

"Pour forth we beseech Thee oh Lord Thy grace into our hearts that we to whom the Incarnation of Christ Thy Son was made known by the message of an angel, may by His Passion and Cross be brought to the glory of His Resurrection through the same Christ our Lord.

"May the souls of the faithful departed through the mercy of God rest in Peace." Amen.

Three times a day, morning, noon and night, the monastery bells had rung the Angelus and each time that Fr. Beppo had recited this prayer during his great number of years in the monastery, he felt that he had drawn nearer to God.

With a light heart he continued his journey even though his steps were heavier for the years that had gone by had taken the lightness of his step and much of the vigor from his body.

Late in the day Fr. Beppo sat down to rest and to partake of the one meal of the day, and as he ate of the black loaf of bread and drank from the spring at hand, he meditated on the mysteries of life.

His mind was not a little disturbed by some things he could not understand, and he was so engrossed in his thoughts he did not hear the approach of a stranger who seemingly had followed in the path pursued by Fr. Beppo.

The good monk was saluted by the traveler who sat down with him and shared the loaf of Fr. Beppo.

The traveler said that he was going the same way and Fr. Beppo told him that he would be glad of his company.

There was something about the traveler that attracted Fr. Beppo very much. There seemed to be a warmth and fragrance coming from him that was very pleasing. Fr. Beppo's weariness had dropped away from him, his step was ever so much lighter, the youth which had fled from him years ago had come back and taken possession of his body. Surely this fellow traveler must have some wonderful charm about him to bring into the heart of Fr. Beppo the joy and gladness that he felt therein. It seemed to him that this old heart of his wanted to sing and to burst forth into melody, proclaiming the beauties of life and the glories that were promised to all who took up their cross and followed Him.

Then the traveler confided to Fr. Beppo that he was an angel in the guise of man. He was a messenger of the Lord on a mission to carry out a divine command.

Fr. Beppo was delighted to be so blessed and they journeyed together, the angel making plain many of the things that had troubled the poor brain of Fr. Beppo.

They came to a great house at nightfall and the angel knocked for admittance and asked for a night's shelter in the name of God. They were brought to the head of the house who greeted them warmly and ordered that rooms be prepared for them and refreshments given to them.

The master of the house like Fr. Beppo seemed greatly attracted to the angel and he ordered the servant to bring to him his great golden cup which he filled with the choicest wines that his house contained, again, and again, for his two guests.

The two travelers were shown to their rooms and after thanking God for his safe journey, Fr. Beppo was soon fast asleep.

It seemed to him that he was asleep but a few minutes when he felt the touch of the angel who bade him arise and continue their journey. As they passed through the banquet room, the angel paused and took the golden cup from which they had been so royally treated the evening before.

Rather a strange return for the kindness accorded him, thought Fr. Beppo, but the angel gave no explanation. All day long they journeyed together Fr. Beppo charmed as ever with the discourse of the angel but ever and again the thought would come to him what a strange return was meted out to the man who had so kindly entertained them the night before.

Late in the afternoon a terrific storm arose, there was a terrible downpour of rain that drenched the travelers to the skin, and there was thunder and lightning that made Fr. Beppo draw even closer to the angel for protection. They must get shelter or perish on the road. A flash of lightning showed them a hut a short distance away and they approached it and knocked for admittance.

A voice demanded who they were and they said "two travelers caught in the storm." They were bade begone and a curse followed the command.

The angel asked in the name of God who was Crucified, for shelter and the voice told them to sleep in the pigsty. The angel thanked him and the two sought rest among the pigs.

In the morning the angel again knocked at the door of the hut and the door was thrown open. The angel thanked the man for his hospitality and gave him as a reward for it the beautiful golden cup which he had taken the night before from the house of the one who had entertained them so well. Then they resumed their journey and ever and anon good Fr. Beppo would rub his poor old head and try to reconcile the action of the angel. The one who had entertained them was punished by stealing his golden cup and the one who had refused them shelter and sent them to sleep with the pigs had been rewarded. Father Beppo would shake his head again, and again.

The third day of the journey the charm of the angel was just as great to Fr. Beppo and the angel confided to him that virtues are much like flowers and they draw forth a fragrance that beautifies and graces those who possess them. Sins are weeds that choke the virtues and must be torn out by the roots that the flowers of virtues grow in the heart.

After the sun went down and the stars came forth, they approached a great castle and the angel knocked for admittance. He told they were two travelers on their way and they sought food and shelter. The lord of the castle himself came down and embraced both of the travelers. He ordered the best rooms in the castle to be placed at their disposal and that the table be laden with the choicest foods and the rarest wines for the refreshment of the two weary travelers. The host entertained the two with stories of his travels and the wars in which he had been engaged. There came forth from the nursery and rushed into the arms of the old man one of the most beautiful children that ever came into this world. She was the granddaughter of the old man and the heiress to all his riches. She sat on his lap while he was telling his adventures and again and again the old man would press her to his bosom showing every evidence of the warmest and deepest love.

By and by the travelers were shown to their rooms and Fr. Beppo on his knees thanked God again for the safe journey which had been given to him and he fell fast asleep while saying the rosary.

Again he felt the hand of the angel bidding him

arise and continue the journey. As they went through the banquet hall the angel turned aside and beckoned Fr. Beppo to follow him into the nursery and there asleep was the beautiful child. The angel whispered into her ear and the most glorious smile that ever adorned the face of an infant came over her features. Then he gently laid his hand on her heart, and the heart ceased to beat, and the child was dead. Then they stole forth from the castle and good Fr. Beppo cried out, "Thou art not an angel of God but of the devil, here we part, you go your way and I go mine, never again together."

"Oh, good Beppo," said the angel, "I am an angel of the Lord and I am doing His work."

"Is it the work of God," cried Beppo, "to basely steal the golden cup from the man who so well entertained us, and is it the work of the Lord to reward the villain who let us perish with the pigs, and is it the work of the Lord to slay the child of he who so lavishly entertained us?"

The angel raised his hand and in front of Beppo's eyes made the sign of the cross. "Beppo," he said, "it is not given to the finite mind to comprehend the work of the Infinite.

"I took the golden cup from the man who entertained us because love of that cup was making a drunkard out of him. I took that cup from him to reward him for his hospitality. Now he will live a sober and just life and his reward will be in Heaven.

"I gave this golden cup not as a reward, but as a punishment to him who denied us hospitality in the name of Christ. He will die a drunkard's death and be punished in everlasting fires."

"Yes, but the child?" asked Beppo.

"Yes, the child is now an angel in heaven. She has

gone to her Maker in all her innocence and with all the original beauty of her soul. The Lord of the castle who entertained us so lavishly, has led a good life and done many heroic acts of virtue, yet his love for this little child, the heiress of all his wealth led him to contemplate doing a great wrong that he might leave her more wealth. To save his soul I sent the child before him into heaven."

Beppo bowed his head and when he raised it again the angel had vanished. From over the hills came the sound of the Angelus bell and the good monk paused to recite the beautiful prayer.

Printed in the USA
CPSIA information can be obtained
at www.ICGtesting.com
LVHW010355010823
753942LV00009B/435